i

PARALLEL LIVES

By

Veronica Lavender

First published   18/3/2009

Second publication 3/4/2014

ISBN: 1497327431

ISBN-13: 978-1497327436

Other books by Author

The Essential Creativity of Awareness

Embrace the Power Within

The Empowered Affirmations Balancing Technique

Jack the Ripper & the Ghost of Mary Jane Kelly.

ACKNOWLEDGEMENTS

I would like to say thank you to my children Debbie, David and Karen, for their continued love and support, they are a great inspiration to me, and I am so proud of them. Thank you to my dear friends for the hours of discussions and encouragement, especially to Caroline for the psychic drawings.

Thank you, to all readers of my first book: The Essential Creativity of Awareness. I have learned so much more, since the publication of my first book, and I hope that it's offered encouragement to anyone pursing their own dreams. Do not be put off from following your dreams, because with determination we can all perfect our gifts, skills and abilities, achieving even more success within our lives.

So I dedicate this book to all who pursue their dreams in earnest, and who have touched my life in so many different ways. Thank You.

Throw a sixpence into a wishing well, what do you wish for, a dream, something you desperately want or are you asking someone else to grant your wish or dream. The only person stopping your dream from becoming a reality is yourself. Flick a sixpence into the air, heads I will, tails I will not, you are then leaving it all to chance. But if you put the sixpence into your pocket as a lucky charm, a reminder that you are promising to make your dreams come true. Or you can give yourself six reasons why you cannot achieve your dreams, then give yourself six reasons why you should. Do not allow your fears to hold you back; do not allow the lack of money or some other reason to hold you back. If you really wanted to achieve your dreams for the right reasons then nothing would stop you.   Good luck!

PREFACE

I was born in Wolverhampton in 1953; I have lived throughout the Midlands area for most of my life. I have three children who have given me the love and inspiration to enable me to seek my dreams. They have blessed me with grandchildren who bring purity, love and joy within my everyday life. My spiritual journey started over 30 years ago, it was a journey of my soul's quest of reinventing and rediscovering my authentic self. With the age of spirituality I have been able to transform my life, enabling me to empower myself, unleashing my limitless potential.

With the new Age of Aquarius I have been encouraged to access my extraordinary gifts, skills and abilities, with the spiritual reawakening of my soul. This has enabled me to become spiritually and self-aware, whilst pursuing my dreams. It gives me the opportunity to explore and experience the many holistic and alternative therapies, along with the paranormal. Once I'd achieved and understood the different methods of releasing the negative emotions and blockages from within, as aided with the reconnection of my higher conscious self. I was then able to access the Akasha records, and Esoteric knowledge and wisdom of long ago. My spiritual pathway had one main purpose; it showed me that it was not just a way of life, but to the different methods of achieving a life, consciously. This has enabled me to find my inner-self, and that of my true-self through the process of spirituality.

My journey at times had been very hard, with challenges that I thought I would never overcome, but with the help of the knowledge about my past lives, I was able to achieve a true picture of my truth, and inner-self. This has allowed me to reinstate balance and harmony within my life, creating peace within my heart and soul. The soul's journey takes many lifetimes to complete, and this has given me the opportunity to overcome the many obstacles within my present life. Sometimes I was so unhappy with certain situations within my life that I actually wanted out of this lifetime. But with divine intervention, I was prevented from doing so in order for me to be able to share my life experiences with others, who are also travelling their own unique journey of their soul's quest. Now I share that knowledge with others, leading us all eventually to the infinite wisdom of all lives.

My personal spiritual journey has allowed me to achieve the freedom, from the restraints and restrictions that I'd created for myself, due to the lack of understanding of why the different negative situations or circumstances had happened to me. The knowledge that came from the in-sight into my parallel lives, gave me the wisdom to know what I could change within my life, and to be more accepting of the things that I could not. My journey into my past lifetimes has now set me free, from the old programming, my negative beliefs and concepts, of thinking that I wasn't good enough in some-way, now living my life to the best of my abilities. Once I'd chosen not to buy into the poor me syndrome anymore, I was able to take back the control of my everyday life. I am now free to be me, the person I've always known myself to be, but without the negative emotional traits of my past, influencing this lifetime. It's a journey that we'll all take one day, in search of our soul's quest in understanding the real reasons behind why we are here, and in all that we do, say and think.

My spiritual journey has enabled me to become a part of the collective consciousness of humankind. It's allowed me to achieve the enlightened state of awareness, granting me the life that I had only dreamed of. With the reconnection to the universal and earth's energies, and my authentic self, has now transformed my life, unleashing my limitless potential of all lifetimes.

INTRODUCTION

Our past lifetimes influence this lifetime, affecting us in so many different ways, and they form part of our characters and inherited traits, making us all unique and individual. They give us our unique personalities, exposing the hidden depths of our characters, allowing us the opportunity to recognise and achieve our full potential. The soul's quest is to experience each incarnation, and to be given the opportunity in understanding our life's lessons. This allows the challenges in life to be recognised and overcome, all being a big part of our life's purpose.

When we have achieved the greater understanding of our life's lessons, will allow us to gain more in-sight and depth, into our true character and of who we've ever been. With exposure to the higher consciousness, and the incredible vibrations of the universal and earths energies, will grant us with our extraordinary gifts, skills and abilities. This would aid us in unleashing our creative talents, enabling us to reach our limitless potential, of all times.

The Age of Aquarius brings new beginnings for us all, but first we must let go of our negative emotions and traits. With this new Age, comes the clearing of the sub-conscious and un-conscious mind of our repressed emotional issues. The negative issues that creates illness, and disease that once released, reconnects us to our higher consciousness once again, allowing us to heal and to become a part of the collective consciousness of mankind. We must all reconnect with our personal inner resources to meet and overcome the challenges in life in order to transform our lives.

We have to have courage to explore the soul's journey that enables us to reconnect with the ultimate power of our truth and true-selves. Allowing us to understand the reasons why the different situations and circumstances have happened to us within our life, and the truth behind our actions or deeds. All life's experiences enable us to continue our spiritual journey of the soul's quest, becoming enlightened with the reconnection of our truth. This would allow our instinctive, and intuitive impulses, and the reactions to life changing experiences, to be recognised and acted upon, allowing us to fulfil our pre-agreed destiny and dreams. When we do not recognise our lessons in life, fate will take a hand in showing us what we need to know, in order to evolve successfully.

Our parallel lives brings our consciousness into the present, and allows our positive future to unfold, helping us to cope with what the future holds by being consciously aware, because we are all going to experience some hard times. Our lives have been thrown into chaos with the earth's magnetic field weakening. It has been predicted that with the reversal of the north and south poles, will greatly affect the earth's energy field, and also the energies of everyone who resides upon this planet. We are all experiencing catastrophic proportions of our world changing, with us coping with natural disasters such as flooding, earthquakes and volcanoes erupting. We are now living in the golden Age of Aquarius with us all participating in the cleansing, purification, and the spiritual transformation of all aspects of ourselves and our world.

We have all at sometime or other, experienced déjà vu memories from other lifetimes, influencing our present life. The memories being relived in our waking or dream state, experiencing strong feelings of people, places and the different circumstances that we feel we've experienced before, but a long time ago. We are all reminded of the events of other lifetimes that we'd pre-agreed to learn from within this lifetime. When we have overcome our life's lessons, the positive vibrations of these lifetimes will then greatly influence all that we do, say or think. This allows us to become our authentic and true selves; we are all required to understand our life's purpose, and to translate the hidden messages or to understand the well kept secrets. The details about our strengths and weaknesses, but more importantly what drives the unrest of our souls, and the real reasons behind our choices or decisions that we've made, and too why we had chosen to make them?

To become whole and complete is about reinstating our positive attributes, and accomplishments of all lifetimes, brings the vibrations of our true-self into this lifetime. Our altered state of awareness then accesses our instinctive gifts, and abilities to use within our everyday lives, but naturally. By accessing the truth would enable us to survive beyond 2012. Which will help us all to unite with the collective consciousness of mankind, enabling our souls to be rejuvenated, where each individual will be empowered with the realignment of the mind, body and soul? But more importantly the reconnection to the universal and earth's energy, connecting us to the creator all that is.

Our past lives are as much a part of us has this lifetime is, and our inherited characteristics, with the unseen force of our sub-conscious mind driving us forwards. All that we need will be provided for, allowing us to understand the importance of our life's purpose and lessons, and how we can overcome them. This helps us all to reinstate balance and harmony within, achieving a higher conscious state that grants us with abundance within all aspects of our lives. This will aid us all in achieving world peace, but first, we must achieve an inner peace that radiates outwards affecting us all. Our soul is connected to and interpenetrates all life, helping us all transcend to the higher conscious realms of universal love, wisdom and truth.

CONTENTS

CHAPTER 1

MY LIFE

My story begins when I was 35 years of age; I was married with three children. My life at that particular time was very busy, and my husband and I had built a business at the same time of raising our three children. Life for me was hectic with very little time to pursue any of my personal dreams or ambitions. Over the years of trying to achieve a balance, between work, wife and motherhood, I found that my life was out of control. All aspects of my life were controlling me and not me, being in control of my life. I started to view my life in the negative sense, resenting different aspects of my life because I did not have time for myself anymore.

I thought that it was selfish to want other things within my life, when I already had so much. From the outside, it looked as if I had everything that you could possibly want within your life. In fact, everything you'd expect from working hard. Even so, I felt that something was missing within my life, and I was unable to understand why I felt so unhappy. The things within my life that I truly did rejoice in were my family life, enjoying our children and all the joy they brought. As with any parent, all we want for our children is the very best from life, so hence the business that we'd built together was with the sole intention of giving us all, a better life and future.

Our parents helped us, firstly with the children then eventually within the business, but soon, we were all totally consumed with the everyday running of a growing business. We had our high times and low times, but we never lost touch with our responsibilities to the children. For me, I had lost touch with the responsibility to myself, no one's fault but my own. So I started the process of procrastination, beating myself up at every opportunity taking advice as criticism, which resulted in me losing my self-worth, confidence and faith in my own abilities. The thing is, we never realise this as so, and it's only becomes evident later on. I had allowed others to put me down; they became too demanding and inconsiderate, not realising that this too, was about their lack of trust and faith in their own abilities, the mirror image of me.

What happened to me I had un-consciously allowed to happen, as it was all part of my life's lessons and purpose. So the negative traits of my learning's had started to influence my life, I felt unhappy all because I had not recognised my own imbalances or the disharmony within. I totally dismissed the inner voice of my soul that was gently trying to guide me forwards. All brought on, by my ignorance to the inner self, and the disconnection from my higher conscious self which created the unrest of my true-self. I got to the point where I did not recognise myself anymore, what had happened to me had left me feeling in a vulnerable state. Leaving me craving for some idyllic time when I felt happier, not realising that all within my life was as it should be, all being part of the divine plan. Then everything within my life changed dramatically, the journey that followed was all that I had pre-agreed too, long ago.

When I was 43 years of age, I went through the pain of divorce, not just divorcing my husband but also the company that we'd built together, along with leaving the matrimonial home. I remember feeling like I had died and gone to hell, well not hell exactly, but a place where the grief and shock was unbearable. My whole life had changed; the enormity of the consequence of my divorce was just too much for me to cope with. The pain that I'd created for myself was so bad, that I wanted out of this lifetime.

The real test in life comes from facing our demon's head on, but at the time I was not aware of the reasons behind the situation that I'd found me to be in. The vital information about my life's purpose was not accessible to me at that time, leaving me in a vulnerable state of confusion of what my life's purpose was all about. The important information that would have saved me from some of the pain and grief that I'd created for me. The details about my life, what would happen to me, and the reasons as to why? Which would have allowed me to be more accepting of the different situations within my life, making everything all right and easier to bear? So let me explain.

I pre-agreed to everything that would happen to me within this lifetime, before I was born. I believe we all made an agreement to the course of events that would happen to us within any lifetime in order to learn from past mistakes. We will have understood the reasons as to why these different situations or circumstances would happen to us, and then be given the solutions to overcome our problems. Also we are given the information about our past lifetimes where we'd created anguish or torment, and hadn't dealt with the emotional issues at the time, causing us unrest within.

Therefore on our death, taking the negative vibration of our emotional imbalances onto the next level of our existence, where we would have gained some understanding. But then, we needed to come back into another lifetime that would allow us to gain deeper understanding to our new life's lessons and purpose. So our journey starts all over again, with the intention of us living our lives, to overcome some important learning's, and the details of that agreement or the memories are locked deep within our sub-conscious at the moment of our birth. Waiting until the time becomes right, for us to search for those memories, and to reconnect with the truth of our true selves. Until then we have to maintain faith, belief and trust in ourselves, accepting our life's lessons as part of the divine plan.

So for me, to be able to accept my demise was to be a big part of my life's lessons and learning's. So having pre-agreed to all the different aspects of my life, I had to wait for the time to become right in order for them to be played out. Allowing me to understand, and overcome the learning's gaining an in-sight into their true meanings. It's because I had not consciously understood the significance of a lesson given in a previous life which then created a disharmonious situation within this lifetime, in order for me to fully understand its true meanings. When we fail to understand what our emotional imbalances are all about, creates the unrest of the soul.

In pursing my inner journey I accessed the information that reinstated my gifts, skills, and abilities that would allow me to attain the greater understanding of my demise. This would enable me to release the imbalance and negativity from within, giving me the opportunity to restore health once I'd fully understood the significance of my learning's within this lifetime. I must say that when that time came for me to understand my life's purpose, I was so joyful to realise that I'd done what I was supposed to do, the choices I made we're the right choices for my learning's.

The in-sight into the divine plan was quite informative, and the reason of what happened to me, I had created for someone else in a previous lifetime? So what we give out, is what we get back, not always within the same lifetime but when the time becomes right for us to gain a deeper understanding of what we needed to learn. So thinking that I was hard done too, was just a state of mind, and with any unhappiness that I'd experienced, I'd only focus on the negative attributes. Later on, when I'd have had a chance to heal, I would then focus on the positive aspects of those learning's.

Our life's lessons are about what we do within our lives, and the underlying reasons behind them. It's also about our hidden agendas, and the real reasons behind our insecurities or negative emotions. The unhappiness that both my husband and I had created for us was about the lack of trust in each other, and our life together. Not realising that there was a bigger picture about our lives, a picture that told a story of long ago. It was a story that held the key to the real reasons of our lifetime together, and to what we could achieve. I can only tell my story, because I only have access to my own personal information of my truth, and to what my life had been all about. But there were lessons that required the both of us to learn; in hindsight we should have learned them together, and not feeling threatened by each other, and the choices that we'd made, but to work together in understanding what was really going on within our lives. We should have been there for each other no matter what, and to overcome our problems together, instead of pursuing other things that had created a void between us.

We have all experienced past lives where only the negative traits are dealt with, maybe time running out before we could really enjoy the fruits of our labours. We would also have had very positive past lives where we successfully understood our lessons, and enjoying the positive aspects of those learning's activating our full potential, enabling us to achieve great things. Until that happens, we can only draw on the vibrations of those positive times in which to help us understand our problems.

So at first, my negativity had kept me in place where I lived my life through the people I loved, all because I was in denial of my own life. Once I had reconnected to the positive vibration of all lifetimes, I then gave myself permission to pursue the reconnection of my inner-self and higher consciousness. The realisation that I was worthy of putting my needs first, helped me restore faith and belief in myself. Granting me with the positive attributes of my higher self, a knowing that once I'd given to myself, I was then able to give to others, successfully.

There is a big difference between giving of you and giving up of yourself. To achieve a balance within all aspects of our lives, will allow us more energy to help others but more importantly, we will know when to offer that help and support. When we are true to ourselves, helping others would become natural and instinctive. Enabling us to be really understanding and to be non-judgemental, only then being able to show love and compassion at all times. To experience love and joy in all that we do, say or think makes our lives so rewarding. This allows us to have a life that just flows, enabling us to accomplish our dreams and desires, effortlessly.

As a child I was happy and carefree, dancing and singing with a love of nature, I felt my happiest when I was outdoors. Through the process of growing up my negative traits were brought into play. So I started to experience the disharmony within, only at the time I did not comprehend what it was all about. I would look to others for love or approval, doing the different things to please and to be noticed. The more I did, the more that was expected from me, making me try even harder all because I felt it was not enough. This was to be the cycle for quite a few years to come; trying to fill the voids within, my void was a lack of love for me.

With me not having self love affected every area of my life, not loving myself enough in order to put myself first, doing things for others, just to prove my love. I did not realise that the lack of love for myself had left me wanting others to show their love for me. But if you do not love yourself, who can? The answer is simple; no-one can but you, this state of unhappiness cost me my marriage. My marriage was not really doomed, it was my pre-destined destiny and I lived the life that I was supposed to live. I had denied others in a past life, so I was being denied in this one. Not necessarily with the same people as I found myself to be within this lifetime, just some of them. But you can be assured that what goes around comes around. The lesson for me was not to put my happiness in the hands of someone else, only I could make myself truly happy by reconnecting with my true self, and that of my truth once more.

Another aspect of that denial was in a previous lifetime, where I'd died in order for someone else to enjoy the fruits of my labour. My negative trait was that I'd not appreciated my life at that particular time. I had work hard and put too much emphasis on the material wealth in making me happy. I had created the unrest and disharmony within my soul, and so I died due to an accident, hence the lesson. It takes us lifetimes to overcome the unrest of our souls, because we are all a product of our negative traits, everyone pre-agreeing to what would happen to them within their lifetime. We agreed to the different situations and circumstances of the lessons that we needed to overcome, enabling us to achieve our life's purpose, in order to fulfil our dreams.

Whatever happens to us within this lifetime is about a configuration of numerous learning's all part of the intricate learning's of our destiny. Allowing us to choose when and how, we would overcome our problems. Bearing in mind, the cause and effect of our actions and to how they will affect the physical body. Also, how it affects our lives with the imbalance or disharmony, creating the mental confusion. All of which, will affect our health if we store the negative undertones of our learning's within, creating us with disharmonious ailments, illness and conditions etc.

In this lifetime I realised that the material trappings would not make me happy, that's why I walked away from everything. Not necessarily for someone else to enjoy what I had worked for, but because it did not make me truly happy. We put too much emphasis on the material trappings, thinking that it would make us feel better about ourselves, with us trying to fill the voids within, instead of concentrating on what we in-fact have! It's only when we lose what we've had within our lives that we realise how much our lives depended on them, and the loss of it, makes us feel vulnerable. Material wealth makes us work hard to maintain the lifestyle we have created for ourselves, believing that it would make our lives more rewarding.

When my husband and I first set off on our new life together we would have lived in a shed as long as we were together. It's strange how your values in life change; we forgot to focus on the things that really mattered to us, all because we were working hard to maintain our lifestyle. My own unhappiness was created because I'd not allowed quality time for myself, consequently having an adverse effect on our relationship because we no longer had quality time together. This puts far too much pressure on maintaining a balance, between motherhood, my relationship and work, and by not recognising the imbalances within, I'd not realised how unhappy I was, until it was too late.

Who I have now become, money cannot buy a vibrational legacy that I can take with me from lifetime to lifetime, and to enjoy on the continuance of my soul's evolutionary journey. The lesson was, I did not deny myself, and I did what I was meant too, not just for me to learn from, but others too. We have both survived the ordeal of the break-up of our marriage, moving onto new adventures. Our memories of our life together, live on within our children and grandchildren, and recorded in time, evolving with us; just in case we need the information of those learning's to prevent us from making the same mistakes, again. But for me, before I had chance to learn my life's lesson, I had remarried and sadly had to learn the lesson all over again. This enabled me to gain an even deeper understanding in no self-worth, low self-esteem, lack of confidence and still, the lack of self-love.

After the break-up of my first marriage, I found myself living on a narrow-boat, trying to recover from the trauma that I found myself to be in. This is when divine intervention stepped in, has I was feeling really vulnerable, unhappy and with no confidence, in-fact in a place that I felt completely alien in. With the break-up of my marriage, moving out of the matrimonial home and the loss of my job had left me in a very vulnerable state of thinking that I had died and gone to hell, and I was being punished for a crime I hadn't committed. Even

I did not recognise myself in this unhappy state; that I wanted out of this lifetime, I just felt I would not recover from what had happened to me. Then one night whilst walking down the towpath, and with the intention of doing what, I really didn't care! Someone spoke to me; he then continued to walk with me down the towpath, only I did not get onto my boat, but his, I wasn't even aware that I had until he asked me to sit down.

I stayed on his boat for two days, later he told me that he'd recognised something within me, and knew what I was thinking of doing. I must have suffered some sort of breakdown but didn't recognise that fact, at the time. He encouraged me to talk, which allowed me the opportunity of trying to understand what had happened to me. It enabled me to slowly pick up the pieces, and start to make decisions about my future, taking one step at a time. I will always be grateful to him because of his encouragement; slowly my life began to turn around and I went off in a new direction, so the process of recovery and healing began. I had no self-confidence what's so ever, and I found myself getting back inside my boat, every time someone walked down the towpath. I would wait until they'd passed before stepping out of the boat again. Being in such beautiful surroundings and enjoying nature, the healing of me gently took place travelling the waterways and learning new skills, allowed my confidence to return, enabling me to enjoy this new adventure and too experience a different way of life.

The gentleman who helped me that night on the towpath became a very good friend; he and his parents had arrived in order to make me a cratch cover for my boat, it was pre-arranged, only I hadn't realised they'd arrived. We then travelled the waterways together in a convoy of boats, meandering through nature at 4 miles per hour, this became my new life, healing and rebuilding my physical, mental and spiritual being. I leant new skills, enjoying the challenges and new adventures of discovering my inner child and self. Who would have thought that I would be handling a 50 foot narrow-boat on my own, let alone reverse it past 20 boats to the water point? I lived on the boat for two years, a small community where people helped each other. With the escapism from the rat race of life and time out to revaluate my life and being given the opportunity to restore my health. My life on the narrow-boat was enjoyed with my children and family, thinking how lucky we were too experience just another of life's adventures together.

Whilst living on my boat was the start of my spiritual pathway, and I soon found myself visiting spiritualist churches, I joined a class to develop my psychic abilities, and also spiritual and self-awareness groups. I enjoyed meeting new people, whilst experiencing the different stages and levels of spiritual growth. I enjoyed the enlightened state of awareness, whilst exploring nature once again, and seeing the world around me with renewed vigour and vitality, and the colours becoming vibrant, I was in awe of my new surroundings. I did meditation with nature all around me, and the vibration of the water had a calming and cleansing effect on my physical self. Meditation allowed me to become more accepting of my new life, and my experience of living on a narrow-boat was a gift from heaven. It's important to acknowledge the rewarding things that we do have within our lives, and we must have a commitment to succeed. It wasn't long before I found myself understanding and then overcoming my lessons, even though it was hard at times, I had to set myself free in order for me to move on with my life.

Whilst travelling the waterways I met my second husband who also lived on a narrow-boat. With my second marriage my husband did an act of a non-selfish nature; he showed me that he thought I was worth all the material wealth that he had. His actions and belief in me placed me on a pedestal, giving me back my self-worth, which worked for awhile, only for the disharmony of my own lack of self-worth, to reappear. His act gave me the opportunity to slowly take back the important attributes of my inner self, but also restored my faith in human nature. He was someone who believed in me, giving me the confidence in my own abilities and belief in myself, enabling me to pursue my dreams. What he saw within me was my strength to succeed, even though I found it hard at times, his encouragement kept pushing me forwards.

The mirror image between us was that I saw within him his vulnerability, and he'd the same strengths as me. He also had the ability to work alone, being self-motivated with a determination to succeed. He brought spontaneity into my life, showing me how easy it was to just go with the flow of life, without the need to anchor myself down by responsibilities that we sometimes place upon ourselves for security. We often tell ourselves that we cannot do this, that or the other, giving a hundred reasons as to why, which keeps us locked into our comfort zone, all because we'd allowed our lives to control us, and not the other way around. Spontaneity gives you adventure, excitement and allows the universe to give you all that you need to survive. It enables you to enjoy your life to the full, giving you the freedom to be able to achieve a balance and harmony between the different aspects of your life.

Our marriage was about us both healing from past trauma, but sadly we were not able to maintain a happy equilibrium, due to the emotional issues that we both had not dealt with from previous relationships, and of the self. At that point I had not dealt with the breakdown of my first marriage, so sadly our marriage came to an end. After the breakdown of my second marriage, I was so distraught; it made me take an even closer look at myself. I felt, I hadn't learned anything from the breakup of my first marriage, so I experienced an emotional state of failure, with me feeling suicidal again, and having the strong emotions of defeat. Not realising at the time that the program I had still running within, was denial of my emotional and physical being, and I felt that I was not destined to be truly happy; I had survived one broken marriage, could I survive a second? I retreated again, back to nature to help heal my wounded spirit.

The journey that followed was hard, because I felt that I would never be able to comprehend what had happened to me or even to understand why. I really did not know what I had done to warrant the situation or circumstances that I'd found myself in. So my inner journey continued, and I felt that I was incapable at that particular time of making any positive choices or decisions or so I thought. Much to my surprise I found the courage to keep moving forwards, it's very difficult when you don't really trust your instincts or decisions. We all do what we have too, in maintaining an outer show of confidence, whilst experiencing inner turmoil.

The secret is to accept what's happening to you, and to try and understand why it's happened? By doing so, you would be able to change the way you'd perceived the situation in the first place. Enabling you, not to take on-board the learning's as a negative, this allows the emotions within not to affect us physically or mentally, but to allow the negative emotions to be dealt with at the time. This gives you the opportunity to release all negative emotions naturally, so that the repercussion of our actions does not create the imbalance or disharmony within. Which if left undetected would create the ailments and illnesses that if left untreated, would eventually cause disease? Affecting not just our busy lives, but in all that we do, and to what we want to achieve. If we are able to comprehend our situation or predicament, we could then alleviate the disharmony within. This helps us to achieve our full potential to improve the quality of our lives, by restoring peace and harmony within; this allowed me, to rediscover my authentic self and true-self whilst continuing the journey of my soul's quest.

I believe that in any lifetime we meet souls who we have infinity with, souls that we have met before, in other incarnate lifetimes. They just seem to come into our lives, to help us out and then disappear again. I am going to refer to them as earthly teachers. I had two earthly teachers who came into my life when I needed them, and they both played an important part in helping me understand aspects of my spiritual pathway.

The first, of my spiritual teachers had always been around me, observing my life but from a distance. When the time became right, he showed me the incredible insights into other dimensions, sharing information that was relevant to my spiritual growth, some of which, I did not fully understand until a lot later on, into my spiritual journey. We had hours of discussions, the power of thought, our actions, and the gifts, skills and abilities that we all have but hadn't recognised as so.

He also shared with me the power of telepathy, healing and the projection of the minds energy and even that of astral travelling. Some of the information given was beyond my powers or ability of that time, going onto really appreciate the unique learning's later on in my life, when I'd pursued my own inner journey of self-discovery. This enabled me to experience the different aspects of my psychic gifts and abilities, allowing me to experience all aspects of the paranormal, and I communicating with spirit.

There was a connection between us, an infinity, we would know what the other was thinking and feeling, sensing their presence when they were near. As quickly as this newfound state of awareness happened it was over, leaving me with an in-sight that encouraged me forwards, even when times were pretty dismal. I have never seen him since, but know that the infinite energy connects our souls together, and when we thinks of me I see a projection of his face before mine. So to my first spiritual teacher and mentor, I thank you.

The next, was quite a few years later, another soul-mate we'd shared a previous lifetime together, again someone that had always been in my life, observing all that I did. When we came together we only spent three months with each other, but the experience blew me away, as I think his experience with me, did the same. When we touched we felt electricity pass between us, I would drain him and he would drain me. We went on an adventure of learning, experiencing first-hand the incredible powers of the unknown.

We visited historical places to feel and experience the different vibrations. We would sense events that had happened in the past, to find that our perceptions was correct when we investigated the details. We would visit art galleries sensing the mood of the artist, when he or she had painted their masterpiece. Projecting us into the paintings, to feel what they may have felt or was feeling at that time of their great work. We would lose ourselves within the music, absorbed in the musical notes, and we enjoyed the experience of becoming the music and sensing the composers' feelings and inspiration. In fact we experienced such a lot that it totally consumed us, so as quickly as it started, it came to an end.

This was one of the most enlightened experiences that I've ever experienced. He is still around today but we are not in touch, we don't need too, for our higher consciousness and infinity with each other, keeps us connected. Whenever I'm in trouble, he's always on the other end of the phone just checking to see if all is well, and often his face his projected to me when I need comfort or guidance. Thank you, to a very dear and trusted friend.

So we all have infinite friends who observe all that we do, whether they are here on the earth plane or have passed over into the spirit world. I believe that we have three such allies in any lifetime; I am looking forward to meeting the next. But if it's not to be within this lifetime, I will meet them once back in the spirit world. A soul mate is not necessarily someone we first marry, but a person who we've shared a lifetime with, and have allowed each other to grow spiritually and personally, overcoming the many obstacles together. Soul mates come together to help and encouraging each other, by not feeling threatened by the choices that the other makes, allowing us both the opportunity to evolve and grow in becoming our own person. We must allow ourselves to be tolerant and kind, but having the courage to know when we are in the wrong and to put it right.

A lesson I wish I'd learnt sooner, rather than later, within this lifetime maybe saving myself from a lot of pain and grief. I soon found myself pursuing the art of kinesiology at the age of 50, (so for those who have not read my first book) kinesiology is the art of muscle testing, a direct response to a particular problem or condition. The process of kinesiology is to work with the higher consciousness, using charts of information that would help us to decipher the hidden truth of our higher self. We would then administer remedies and affirmations which helped with the realignment to our energy field, and that of the physical, emotional, mental or spiritual bodies.

The objective was to track down the root cause, to all of our problems within. Which would allow us to unblock the negativity from within that causes the restraints and restrictions, within our everyday lives? This enables us to elevate not just the imbalances and disharmony within this lifetime, but previous lifetimes also. Not in the order of incarnate years, but into the sequence of events, at the age of when the events happened, as opposed to what century, they happened in.

Some of my lessons within this lifetime were about the elimination of my negative traits of my action and thoughts, and also the understanding of my past lifetime lessons. These lessons Id failed to learn within other lifetimes, and so became part of my life's purpose and understanding. The hardest lesson was the lack of a relationship with myself, with had created a lack of self-love which left me struggling within my life. So I'd pre-agreed to go through all that I'd experienced within this lifetime, in order to understand my life's purpose

15

and lessons that I didn't learn from long ago, and to reinstate self-love within this lifetime.

I gained an in-sight and understanding of my root problem in order to release the tears of the negative emotions of my learning's from long ago. I tried the different holistic methods to overcome my issues by gaining the knowledge and wisdom of what I'd allowed to happen to me. It was a slow process, and at times it was painful to admit to the emotional issues or negativity I'd held within, and the way I'd perceived the different situations or circumstances within my life. My insecurities, and the pride and ego played a big part in keeping me locked into the different negative situations within my life. When I was ready to face the truth about my life's lessons, and to what they were all about, I was then able to release the negativity that I'd held within.

Only when we have achieved the understanding to our problems, do we then appreciate all that we have been through. So my life's purpose was about me reconnecting with my true self, inner self and that of my higher conscious self that holds the truth within its collective consciousness, all that I've achieved or accomplished since time began. The re-establishment of those attributes is my limitless potential that will make me whole and complete, has I continue on my life path by recognising and reinstating them. I rejoice in all that I do have within my life now, and to whom I have become, because I empower myself to be the best I can be.

CHAPTER 2

PAST LIVES

Our past lives play an important part in which we really are, and they form parts of our characteristics and inherited traits. There will be people, who will not comfortable with the theory of us having past lives. This is purely each person's own choice, but it doesn't hurt us to stay open minded because it would benefit us if we allowed ourselves to be open, to the bigger picture of our truth.

Everyone of us at some time or other has experienced Déjà vu memories from long ago, and we have all experienced the instant feeling of knowing someone that we've just met, having an infinite attraction. We have dreamed of places that we have never been too; in fact we've had visions within our dream and waking state, with memories being relived of some forgotten time. We have also experienced skills and talents that have come naturally to us, but also our vacation when suddenly we find a job that is second nature to us. Offering us with contentment and feeling fulfilled, enjoying every aspect of our lives.

Our past lives give us an in-sight into our true-selves, revealing hidden messages and the secrets to our present lifetime. These important in-sights allow us to gain the valuable information that would allow us to fully understand what our lives are all about. They help us to evolve with the continuance of the soul's quest, helping us to become whole and complete once more. The information about our past lives helps us to reinstate equilibrium within our everyday lives, allowing us to realign to the positive attributes of our past lives, because within every past life that we address the more in-sight into our true-selves, and that of our characters.

We have all come into this lifetime, to overcome important lessons that would set us free, from the restraints and restriction that we've found ourselves to be in. We all have problems within our lives, we sometimes find ourselves making the same mistakes over and over again. Have you ever stopped to wonder why you keep attracting the same negative situations or circumstances? Thinking you'd solved the problems within your life only to find that you'd not, leaving you wondering why? When all you've been trying to do is overcome them.

We often find ourselves becoming frustrated or angry, because we cannot understand what it was all about, leaving us feeling perplexed. We then find that the negative undertones of our feelings have created an imbalance or disharmonious situation within. Which if left undetected would create the ailments, illness and eventually the diseases that we suffer from? Our past lives are about the imbalances that we've created for ourselves over the different centuries. We have allowed the emotional condemnations of our learning's to affect our minds, body and soul, on the deeper fundamental levels, of our Being.

With every incarnation that we have, and at the moment of death, the vibration of our mindset is what we take with us. Throughout our lifetimes, we are given the many opportunities to understand our demises. So depending on what we expose ourselves too, will denote in our understanding of the problems, and to the different situations or circumstances that we find ourselves in. If we allow our misperceptions to go undetected we take the risk of creating the unrest within our souls, we have to take responsibility for our actions and the outcome to any situation, good or bad.

The Cause and Effect of our decisions or actions, do not just affect us but others also. What we do unto others we will have done to us, whether in this lifetime or at some other time. But we can be assured that our present lifetime is about the karmic debt of a past-life situation, and they give us the opportunity to learn our life's lessons on a deeper level of understanding which will allow us, to live our lives to the full.

So I pursued my soul's quest with the art of kinesiology and past-life regression. I was able to learn a lot about the lives that I'd previously had, and has I dealt with the negative emotions from these lives that once I'd understood I was able to release the negativity. Once I'd acknowledged how the negativity had affected not just my physical body but the mental pressure of trying to work the different situations out, had caused the negative imbalances within. I realised that I had to be deal with the imbalances on a physical, mental and spiritual level as well as this enabled me to receive a long term understanding and healing of my issues or problems. On releasing the imbalance or disharmony from within, I was then able to bring the positive attributes of those learning's into my daily life.

This healing process gave me an even greater awareness of what I'd done to myself, realising that I'd stored the negative emotions within, which had created the physical ailments and illness in the first place. With any past-life that we address, we often start with the life that has the most negativity or imbalances to be dealt with first. This is because of the lessons within those lifetimes are about our life's purpose within this life. We then address our more positive lives, because the vibrations of which becomes our full potential with us eventually becoming our limitless potential as we consciously grow. So the purpose of each incarnation is to overcome our life's purpose, and to recognise our unrealised potential, enabling us to become a limitless Being.

I have listed some of my past lives below, with my learning's of the different situations that I needed to overcome as part of my life's purpose. The age of when my imbalance or disharmonious situation occurred and to what I was required to overcome. But also the most important learning's which

19

made a huge difference, with the way I then started to perceive my life to be. Interestingly, the age I was in the previous life, I was of a similar age within this life, when the disharmony within, presented its self to me.

1943AD. I was a chorus girl aged 46yrs. I was married with three children. I was murdered, strangulation. Why? Because I had felt like a victim, so therefore I became a victim. The scenario of feeling hard done too, having to struggle in life, with very little resources to the point where I gave up on life. (Remember I had agreed to this lifetime, as with all lifetimes, there are a lot of factors to be taken into consideration, before our fate is decided). This was a representation of the overall learning's which resulted in my demise. Every one of us has different learning's; we are all responding to our own hidden a-genders. So what happened to me does not necessarily mean, it will happen to you, even if you think you have a similar mindset. We are all unique, so the lesson was that I felt hard done too, because I found myself in a position of poverty. In this lifetime I nearly allowed the same situation to destroy me, when I had the material and financial wealth taken away, and I had to start all over again. The lesson I learned was, to have Faith, Belief and Trust in myself, and to provide for all my needs, but also to be responsible for myself and my welfare, achieving my dreams and self-love. After my death from this lifetime, I was reborn into the same century in 1953.

1868AD. I was male aged 46yrs. I lived in London; and I was married with no children. When my wife died I became a recluse, I gave up on life, and I felt that I had nothing left to live for. So at the age of 62 I died with that mindset. The lesson was about me living my life through others, so they became a projection of what I wanted for myself. On learning this valuable lesson, I now live my life for myself.(Interestingly, my mother who has been on her own for 9 years has also given upon life after my father died, and she lived her life

20

through her children and husband) this is a lesson that I chose to learn from my mother, within this lifetime.

1776AD. I was female aged 44yrs. I lived in a place called Appleby Magna near Measham. I was a white witch, but was drowned because of my beliefs. I worked with flower and herbal remedies. The lesson that I learned was that I was a threat and feared by those who controlled others. Even into day's age, there are those who still fear the unknown; because when any individual explores their own spiritual journey they end up taking back the control to their everyday life, and infinite power. (Two of my dear friends from this particular lifetime, are with me within this lifetime, we are all spiritually working together) this has allowed us to pursue our beliefs that are more readily accepted in this cyclic Age of Aquarius, where we are all being given the opportunity to transform ourselves consciously and embrace the golden opportunities of this new age.

1560AD. I was female aged 50yrs. I was living with my partner who died with his head in my lap from alcoholism. At that moment I realised how much I'd loved him, but also felt guilty, thinking I could have done more for him. So when I died at the age of 60yrs, it was with the mindset of guilt and grief (inner crying). The lesson that I learned was that I could not have done anything to save him, because we all have a responsibility to ourselves, in maintaining a healthy mind, body and soul. We are all responsible for the situations or circumstances that we find ourselves in, a product of our own doing. In this lifetime the lesson was to learn how to alleviate any emotional imbalance or disharmony from within, because if left undetected would create physical problems, conditions, illness and diseases, later on in life. To understand the Cause and Effect of our actions and perception to the demises that we find ourselves in, would help in elevating the imbalances that would then help us to achieve healthy lives. For me the inner crying was about ignoring those imbalances within, saying I was alright when I clearly was not. The inner crying of

21

not letting the positive emotion of grief or guilt takes its proper course. With procrastination of the choices or decisions that I made, thinking that I was wrong in some-way caused me to suppress the negative emotions. Instead of being able to accept that things were, as they were meant to be. (This partner is with me in this lifetime, the learning's are still going on today).

1458AD. I was female age 45yrs. I died in a horse and carriage accident. I was living a life of denial of my situation, not taking responsibility for myself in anyway. I was incapable of making any decisions, leaving it up to others to make decisions or choices for me. I denied myself Physically, Emotionally, Spiritually and mentally, becoming a victim to my negative mindset. The lesson I learned was, not to deny myself on any level of my being, and to take responsibility for myself. We do have choices and everything we need is provided for, to enable us to live our lives successfully, hence my inner journey. It's to have Faith, Trust, and Belief in us, and to be Accepting of all things good or bad. We cannot change what has already happened but we can change the way we continue on our life's pathway. (Interestingly, the injuries sustained in the accident were weak areas within my physical body in this lifetime. Muscular aches and pains to the left hand side of my body and neck, once I'd addressed this lifetime, all my ailments disappeared completely).

1330AD. I was female age 25yrs. I lived this lifetime without the use of my spiritual gifts, being in awe of my grandfather who was very wise and spiritually minded. I learned a lot from him, but chose not to use my spiritual gifts within that lifetime, all because I was happy as I was and I didn't need too. This life was about trusting the positive influences that my grandfather had over me; he guided me successfully through life. (Interestingly my grandfather was actually my father within this lifetime, and he too, decided not to use his spiritual gifts this time around. Even though he was very knowledgeable, he could not comprehend the bigger picture of life.) Sadly my father is no longer with us, but offers great support to me from the other side. The lesson was to stay open to the bigger picture of life, and to be fully in my life, and not just simply doing things within them just to get by, but also to be connected to the higher vibration of my inner-self, truth and consciousness.

1157AD. I was female age 26yrs. In this lifetime I felt disconnected from life, a feeling of indifference to what was going on around me, holding onto the past and not allowing my life to unfold naturally. I was always looking at life from the outside, never feeling connected to others, and it was a life of constant battles, I withdrew from life turning in on myself, creating an inner pain which caused me to have an illness, and eventually a disease which resulted in my death at the age 46yrs. The lesson I learned was to be connected with my inner-self, and that of my truth, as this would have allowed me my natural path through life. It would also have enabled me to be accepting of all things within my life, but more importantly connected to the higher vibrations where I would have accessed all that I needed to live abundantly within that lifetime. I should have been more trusting of myself and my abilities.

835AD. I was female age 24yrs. In this lifetime I was murdered in order for someone else to step into my shoes and live my life. I was stabbed in the back so I didn't know who had killed me. (Interestingly, when I was going through the break-up of my first marriage, and with the course of events that happened to me, plus being denied of what I had worked hard for. I did feel like I'd been stabbed in the back, and someone else did benefit from my hard work). The lesson learned was that we all have choices, and the choices that I made allowed others to take it all from me. In 835AD that is exactly what happened, I put myself in a position where someone took my life from me.

All of the above past lifetimes were about the lessons that I had pre-agreed to learn within this lifetime, hence my life's purpose. Once I had learned and overcome the lessons, I was then able to draw down the positive attributes of those lifetimes into this one. Within any lifetime that we've had, there would have been aspects that were negative and needed to be dealt with, before we could draw or focus on the positive aspects of those lifetimes. We have also had many other lifetimes that were very positive and rewarding. It doesn't matter what we have within our lives or to whom we share our lives with, the secret is to live our life joyfully and to only see the good in everything. We should all live everyday as though it was our last, never putting off till tomorrow what can be achieved today, and it's important to be only living in the Now! I will now tell you about the past lifetimes where I was blissfully happy and successful.

376AD. I was female, and I had a very positive lifetime where my vibration, skills and abilities was used to help others, the consultations I gave earned gave me a high standard of living. I was very happy, enjoying every aspect of my life, being contented in all that I did.

620BC. I was female, and I had a very positive lifetime, I used the art of muscle testing similar to kinesiology, again enjoying my life to the full. It doesn't matter what we have within our lives but to how we perceive them, showing gratitude and rejoicing in all we do. The secret is to live our lives in love, light and joyfulness; this allows us to see only the good in everything and everyone. We are then able to appreciate our life which makes us responsible for our Well Being.

5300BC. I was male and again I experienced a positive life, as I was happy and content in all that I did. In this life I was an Egyptian working on the temples, and I died due to some dispute that cost me my life. I was buried alive; this was my natural time to die. Within this lifetime we had high vibrations, but our Halo's were no longer visible to the naked eye. We were connected to the higher vibrations that allowed us to achieve incredible things. Interconnecting with all aspects of life, which brings together the universal and earth's energies, these energies or vibration allows us to receive all that we need in order to achieve great things. We had incredible powers and in-sight into the unknown forces of our creation.

8700BC. I was female, and we were of a high vibration, but our Halo's had almost disappeared. This was also a happy and contented life, living my life to the full. It was a modest life and when it was over, I returned happily to the spirit world.

12,000BC. I was female, and we were of a high vibration our Halo's slowly disappearing. I was accepting of all aspects of my life, experiencing the adventures and challenges of life willingly. I overcame my lessons in life gracefully. We do not have to have material or financial wealth within our lives in order to be blissfully happy, it's about what we do have that's important and the people we share them with. It's important to give thanks for the simple pleasures of life, and the people we hold so dear, loving them unconditionally.

36,000BC. I was female, and our halos had just started to disappear. This was a successful and rewarding life, enjoying abundance and fulfilment. The loss of my life was due to an accident, this was my natural time to return to the spirit world. In acceptance we would not fear death; we would accept our death as a continuation of life, with us just moving onto the next level of our existence.

47,000BC. I was female, and had a visible halo. I was blissfully happy and content. I lived the life that was intended, returning to the spirit world when it became time for me to do so naturally. Even in a positive life we have to make sure that we continue to learn and not allow our vibrations to lower. This only happens when we allow our insecurities to allow us to attach ourselves to the lower physical level of our existence, of thinking that we need things outside of ourselves in order to feel better about whom we really are.

55,000BC. I was female, and had a halo. I was blissfully happy and content, again living the life that was intended. I died at the age of 42 years, fighting for a cause that I believed in. When we follow our hearts and believe in ourselves totally, we have trust, honour, loyalty and respect, knowing that we are being our truth at all times.

85,000BC. I was male, and had a halo. I was blissfully happy and content; I enjoyed a life of wealth, dying naturally when the time came for me to return to the spirit world. When living in a time where our vibrations were high, this allowed the negativity within life to be counteracted naturally.

100,000BC. I was female, and had a halo. In this lifetime I enjoyed great wealth, a charmed life except for my relationship where I was not allowed to marry for love, but status. The lesson learned was I should have been more accepting of what I did have within my life, as opposed to fighting against it, because by not doing so I didn't realise that I love my husband until it was too late. Within this life I'd done just that! Because years after my divorce from my first husband I realised how much I still loved him, even though it was too late to do anything about it, because we'd both moved onto other relationships.

In 100,000BC we all had Halo's visible to the naked eye, living in peace and harmony. We all had high vibrations, connected to our higher selves and the consciousness. We were also connected to the Universe and Mother Nature, where we lived in Unity with humankind. By 36,000BC our Halo's began to disappear, due to the fact that the disharmony had started to affect each individual. By 5,300BC our Halo's were no longer visible to the human eye. We still had a high vibration but not enough to allow our Halo's to be visible.

Through time and the many centuries our vibrations became so depleted that we now live in a world of human suffering, and with the unrest of the nation leaving us at times, struggling with the different aspects of our everyday lives. We are all affected by the world's mass-negativity.

The Twenty-first century is upon us; with the reawakening of spirituality. We are all being put on notice, to do things that can alter the course of history, and the distinction of our planet. Maybe we've left it too late for our planet, but not for ourselves. It's never too late to raise our vibration, that's why we are all pursing a more spiritual pathway, in order to understand where each and every-one of us went wrong, giving ourselves the opportunity to be able to put it right. When we understand and alleviate the negativity from within, not only do we alter the level of our own consciousness, but also the level of the collective conscious awareness worldwide?

Jesus was sent to earth in order for us to learn and to find our way back to the times when the collective vibration of our creator and universe was evident within us all. It was a time when we lived in perfect peace and harmony, granting us with contentment and abundance within our lives. Our higher consciousness accessed our gifts, skills and abilities that were instinctive and pleasurable. A vibration where miracles did happen allowing us to live blissfully within our chosen lifestyles. We all have the natural gifts of healing, and we must use our mystical gifts, skills and abilities to the highest good of all. I learned the art of kinesiology back in 620BC, it probably was not called kinesiology but the art of muscle testing was used to alleviate the problems that created the imbalances within, they also used herbal remedies as a possible way of elevating illness or disease.

Over the many centuries we've used alternative and holistic techniques or remedies, aiding in maintaining health, wealth, and happiness with realignment to the mind, body and soul. This granted us with all that we needed to fulfil our life's lessons and purpose, allowing us to achieve our dreams, successfully, but more importantly to unleash our limitless potential of all lifetimes.

My life's journey so far, has led me into the many aspects of the unknown; it's opened doorways into other dimensions of the paranormal. I find it all fascinating exploring the philosophy of life, which has brought interesting people into my life, making my life so enriched. My life's journey so far, has given me back my personal power and control, and I make choices or decisions freely now, and I'm not afraid to admit that I may be wrong, then being able to change course if I need too. I no longer feel threatened by other people's decisions or choices, knowing that we are all right, in what we say, think or do. To be accepting releases us from the restraints and restrictions that we all hold us too at times!

We are all travelling our own unique pathways, in search of the truth. But the most rewarding gifts to give the self, is the opportunity to gather that infinite knowledge and wisdom together, helping each other along the way. When we are fully connected to the family of life, we achieve things easily together, with us helping each other along the way, and with communication we all learn so much more.

CHAPTER 3

JOURNEY INTO THE UNKNOWN

When I first started my spiritual journey, I was very afraid of the unknown, often jumping at my own shadow. As a child, I often saw faces on the wall in my bedroom, my parents telling me it was just my imagination. All through my childhood years I had feelings of being watched, often seeing dark shadows of someone walking around the room, even while watching television with my family. I was afraid to go upstairs on my own, let alone go to bed.

I am sure this is a familiar story of most childhood memories. I was always sensitive to people and places, also my thoughts and feelings; never really feeling connected to others. Over the years the sensitivity increased, I always felt that I was looking at life from the outside, never quite fitting in some-how. Observing what was going on around me, whilst people watching, often wondering what their feelings or thoughts were? Not really knowing what life was all about, wondering if others too, felt the same way as I did of not really knowing what was expected from us.

I did not like to be left on my own, especially at night, and whilst visiting my grandmother, who lived in a big house to accommodate her thirteen children, I hated going upstairs; there was a spooky feeling, and a cold spot along the corridor which lead to my Aunties bedroom who was bed-ridden. I would have nightmares and times of anguish, now understanding that what I felt then was not a nice feeling. It was not inviting, seeming to resent my presence in some-way. My mother grew up in this house, and later in life she told me that she had felt the same, scared to walk along the corridor to her own bedroom. Even after I got married and my husband was away on business, my younger sister always came to stay with me because I struggled to stay on my own at night afraid of the dark shadows, sensing things that I couldn't see. This went on for years, even after I'd had my own children, my sister continued to keep me company.

When I was 28 years of age, I learned the art of meditation; this was the start of my journey into the unknown. Meditation was a Godsend; it allowed me to explore my inner self, a journey that is still going on today. Once I had connected to my inner-self, I could set about alleviating my imbalances from within. All brought on by the lack of understanding of what I had done to myself, through no trust, faith or belief in myself. I beat myself up, procrastinating because I had become fearful, anxious and in denial of my true-self, thinking I was wrong in some-way, and being afraid that I was not good enough. I became frustrated with the situations and circumstances that I found myself in; all because I could not comprehend there true meanings.

We all spend a lot of time worry about things that we have no control over. Realising there was nothing to fear except our own negative emotions and insecurities. The disharmony that I felt within was created over years of self-doubting? So it was about understanding the extent of the negative imbalances which I'd created for myself within. This included a lot of ailments, aches and pains, feeling tried and blocked at every turn. To try and understand what it was all about was trial and error at first, with me trying to gain an in-sight into my problems, and to how I could alleviate them. But once I'd understood the imbalances and to what had caused them, I was able to clear the negativity away. This left me feeling revitalized; I then began to have a lot more energy and confidence in the decisions that I made, allowing me to continue with my everyday life, with renewed vigour.

I started to find more time for meditation which was a life saver within my busy life, has it gave me more energy and patience to deal with my every-day life. I would sit and meditate even though the children were playing or running around. Often talking to them, even though my eyes were closed I was in a meditative state, still receiving the unique benefits. I was able to take life in a more relaxed manner, not stressing myself out by the constant battles of trying to achieve balance between the different aspects within my life, a life that was really very demanding.

I continued to visit the spiritualist church, this was a fascinating time has I watched the mediums or clairvoyants give members of the audience messages from the spirits of their deceased loved ones. But what I was really in awe of was being able to see the spirit people standing behind them. Seeing them at first in black and white then maybe a year later, I saw them in colour. To watch the spirit people trying to communicate with the medium was incredible; they waited patiently until the medium had passed on their messages. Then I would see the spirit entity standing by the side of their loved one who had just received the message. For me this was an very exciting and rewarding time.

The messages always offered words of love, comfort and support, giving evidence of continued life after death. Albeit in another dimension, for life is eternal. I had received evidence that my own father was still watching over me, taking an interest in the things that I was doing, encouraging me forwards. Also I received messages from my grandmother, and different family members, some of who had died a very long time ago. Not always understanding the message given, but when the information had been checked by a relative or someone who knew of the person that was giving the message, the details were always proven to be correct. I once witnessed a lady receiving a message from her little girl who had drowned in the canal, the medium gave evidence of what the girl had been wearing, what her favourite toy was, and that the mother's own mother who had also passed to the other side years earlier was looking after the little girl, and that they were both alright. This gave the mother tremendous comfort knowing that her little girl was not on her own, and had adjusted well with the transition to the other side.

Then I learned the art of hands on healing, joining a group of healers on a weekly basis, talking to and placing of the hands upon the many people whom came. Realising that the main purpose was about the art of communication, someone to pay attention to what they had to say, and then giving words of encouragement. When we placed our hands on someone with just a gentle touch, spoke volumes as well as allowing the healing vibration to work its magic. The elderly, when living on their own, and having no-one close enough to offer comfort or support when they were feeling ill or at a low ebb, that at times all they needed was just to be touched. Loneliness or unhappiness creates ailments and illness because we are deprived of the contact with others. Anyone feeling alone or even to feel deserted or abandoned needs contact with others. It's important to our welfare to be held and touched. All it takes is someone to say that they understand what's happening to them, and then offer love, support and encouragement.

To give hands on healing is a gesture that we all do naturally when someone close to us is ill or struggling with life. A mother will automatically soothe and heal her child, when they are ill or in distress. Everybody has healing abilities, something that is not always evident. To be able to heal others properly, you have to reconnect with the inner self and your higher consciousness which allows you to administer self-healing first. Then your higher conscious vibration enables you to heal others, who are less fortunate than yourself. To give healing to others allows them to understand the process of how the healing energy works, giving them a positive approach to self-healing by becoming more body aware, and then tapping into the collective consciousness of humankind where all that we need is within us all.

32

I then moved onto the different development classes, sitting in circle, learning how to communicate with spirit. We sensed the different situations of events that had happened in the past. Learning the art of psychometry which is sensing the vibration of an object, and also the opening of the third eye, understanding the importance of the symbols, and visions that we experienced. We were able to give messages to those eager to hear from their deceased loved ones, and we became a channel to the higher vibrations in order to communicate with all properly. A vibration that allowed us to communicate with our deceased loved ones, with the purpose of passing on their continued love and support, giving evidence of life after death. Sitting in a rescue circle, where we helped lost souls move onto the higher realms. Souls who had become earth bound all because they had not realised that they had died or were in need of reassurance. Sometimes they had not moved on, because they'd unfinished business that needed to be done or maybe they just needed to accept their demise, and be able to say goodbye to their loved ones.

I joined self-awareness classes where I became more aware of myself, and was able to understand my life's purpose or lessons, allowing me to gain an in-sight into the unique workings of the mind, body and soul. Years later I started my own self-awareness classes, helping others to understand for them, and the lessons that they also needed to learn. This allowed them to open up to their higher consciousness, reconnecting them to their own innate knowledge and wisdom. Then I started to run workshops on the numerous subjects of spirituality, experiencing the different holistic techniques, cultures and their unique benefits.

We also learned how to locate our own imbalances within, being able to understand the problem or root cause, elevating the negativity that caused the disharmony. We used different alternative methods, such as the power of colour, crystals, angel cards or flower remedies. Reading self-help books and putting into practice meditational exercises in

33

alleviating stress and tension. The real learning's took place when working closely with our spiritual guides; helpers and deceased loved ones. We pushed our boundaries into the most unbelievable phenomenal experiences, at times disbelieving the extraordinary experiences of the unknown.

When the spiritual doctors started to work through me was an incredible in-sight, I allowed myself to be used as a channel for spiritual healing? Sometimes feeling that I had levitated as the doctors drew close and administered the healing, working through my aura. Seeing their hands transposed onto my own, receiving messages to pass onto the person being healed, in helping them to understand their illness or disease, we sometimes experienced miracles of them being cured. This was about them understanding and receiving what they had already pre-agreed too, all being part of their life's path in understanding how powerful we all can be when administering self healing.

To witness and experience this incredible phenomenon was a very rewarding time, making me realise that we all needed to play our parts in attaining Well Being was to be open to the higher vibration of our life force energy. I then started to explore other boundaries into absent healing; the thought is the deed. Going on to understand that whoever needed healing, all they had to do was to expose them to the higher healing vibration. But first, they must agree to the healing and secondly be open to receiving it.

Healing is achieved through the higher conscious self, and of the higher consciousness of the person that seeks the healing. When healing is given on a higher conscious level, miracles can be performed, but to receive a miracle you have to know that you deserve a miracle, and that you're open to receiving one. So whether it's in the conventional medical ways or the alternative techniques and remedies that you seek, it's important that healing is given to the mind, body and soul. We all have a responsibility to ourselves, to seek the help we need, but first we must be in a position of understanding why we have the problem or condition in the first place. This understanding allows us to be healed on the higher levels of consciousness, healing the mind, body and soul, so that the illness or disease is completely cured. This process allows a shift in our conscious awareness, so we can achieve well being throughout our lifetime.

We are all influenced by our past lives where we may have experienced illness or disease and we have the negative vibration still within us and may require attention. All being part of our life's purpose in understanding and overcoming the negative issues from previous lifetimes, where we have created ailments that we didn't fully understand but were a direct result from emotional issues that we had stored within us. We need to understand the psychology behind our imbalances or disharmony of our ailments, illnesses or disease, in order to achieve a Well Being state, on all levels of the mind, body and soul. Whether they were created within this lifetime or other lifetimes, we need to release the negativity in order to learn from.

The incredible in-sight into the higher self is about all that we do, must be about our highest good, and to the highest good of all concerned. Every-one of us can heal, whether it's others or ourselves, healing to our level of conscious ability. The more we travel our unique soul journeys the more healing vibration that we expose ourselves too, increasing our conscious awareness and healing abilities. We act as a channel for the divine and universal energies, a collective vibration of incredible power of intention. Which allows us to undo all that we had perceived wrongly or did not fully understand in any lifetime that we've had? Hence our life's purpose is to set us free, allowing us to reach our unrealised potential.

Then I went on; to communicate and bring my own spiritual guide's closer because until we reconnect with the higher consciousness our guides they just observe what we do. They try to influence us through our thoughts or feelings, but in communicating with them we are able to understand and achieve a lot more. With their help and guidance, I was able to understand my unique gifts and abilities, also the different aspects of my higher self. I always asked for protection when pursuing and experiencing the different meditational adventures, such as out of body experiences, astral travel, and projection of the mind's energy. All of which expanded my conscious gifts, skills and abilities.

My spiritual journey was quite extensive, experiencing something new all the time, but also to experience them within the different situations of my everyday life. Quite mind-blowing at times, but again we were never exposed to too much at one time, because we would not have been able to cope with the vibration of these incredible phenomenon all at the same time. The main purpose of my guides was to give me the love and support, protection and continued guidance, for my spiritual growth. As I evolved, so did my guide, when I moved up to the next level of conscious awareness, a new guide step in? All of the guides that I've ever encountered are still with me today, but depending on what I am doing to which guide works with me. They've helped me to evolve successfully, because they all hold important relevant information about me that allows me to achieve my limitless potential.

So whether I am meditating or running some workshop, my spiritual guides gather close. I call upon the guide that can help me with the task that I am about to do, it may-be purely for confidence or just support. They are the masters of the task that I have chosen to do and help me complete it successfully. Even when experiencing some spiritual phenomenon, they never interfere unless I ask them too, allowing my gut reactions and instinctive abilities to guide me, accordingly. It is about my higher consciousness allowing me to work to the best of my ability; if I trust my higher self I would always achieve incredible things. So my guides just allowed me the space and time, to learn my lessons whilst experiencing the different aspects of spirituality. This process as allowed me to gain a deeper understanding into my life's purpose, achieving my gifts and abilities, but at my own pace and time. If I allowed my guides to take control, I would never learn. But with their continued guidance and inspiration, I was guaranteed to learn a lot quicker, with less pain or grief.

I have included some psychic drawings of a few of my guides: they are my main guides for the present time, and they change as I evolve and spiritually grown. Ahue, a mandarin, is my door keeper he has been with me for a long time. Ahue's role as my doorkeeper is with the intention of overseeing any communication and exposure into the spiritual realms. He acts as my protector, advices me and supports my spiritual growth. When I was fearful or at times of anguish he always made his presence felt, I would then know that I was not alone, and took strength and support from him.

Ahue became my spiritual mentor, guiding me through the many meditational journeys that I've experienced, keeping me safe and protected at all times. I have seen Ahue only once; it was to be just a one off experience, as it takes a lot of energy for them to show themselves properly to us. I was in awe of him and privileged for the opportunity, the day that he showed himself to me, he'd stood in front of me, and he looked so human and alive. I am truly grateful to my spiritual doorkeeper and friend. If ever you need help or guidance, all you have to do is ask for the help, they never let you down. The way they help you, may not always be in the way that we hoped for, but if you allow yourself to be open to receiving the love, support and guidance, you will receive the help you need.

Ahue
mandarin

Cordice
Ambition

The first is my main guide, his name is Ahue, and he is a mandarin. He has been with me from the beginning of my spiritual journey and life, he often wears a purple and blue robe with big wide sleeves, and his arms are crossed over with his hands tucked inside the sleeves. His moustache is as long as his hair and he is my doorkeeper, watching and overseeing my spiritual journey.

Next is my guide Matteu, he is a monk; again he has been with me from the beginning of my spiritual journey. He helps me with the reawakening of my intuitive and instinctive gifts, skills and abilities. He controls the vibrations that I expose myself too, accompanying me on my spiritual journeys. His robe is dark brown, but occasionally shows me the different colours that aids with my continued spiritual growth.

Caroline N douise matron

Jenny

Caroline Robinson

Next is Jenny, she is a matron, she helps me with healing, overseeing the different doctors working through me. When I first started to become a healer I always used smell ether. She also advises me on a personal level, offering guidance and support.

Martha
sister of mercy

Caroline
Robinson

Next is Martha, she is a sister of mercy. I became aware of Martha about ten years ago when I was going through some very difficult times. She inspired me with a knowing, and to have faith, belief and trust in myself. You just have to look at her stature to know she is all knowing and instils unconditional love.

41

petro
philosopher

Carolyne
Robinson

The last one, is my philosopher Petro, he has been with me for about fifteen years, ever since I wanted to write my first book. He inspires and encourages me, even though he has his work cut out with my lack of intellect. But he does not judge me, for he knows that I am working to the best of my abilities and towards achieving my unrealised potential.

The psychic drawings were drawn by my dear friend; she was a very talented lady, and her medium-ship and clairvoyance as helped many people who are in search of evidence of life after death.

The next part of my journey was to understand the Knowledge and Wisdom, with every new in-sight pushing me to the next level of awareness? Taking me out of my comfort zone at times, which allowed me to achieve new depths of consciousness? No harm every came to me, other than my own projection of fears. With the knowledge and wisdom came the spiritual philosophers, inspiring what I said, did or thought. I often found myself saying things that I could not possibly have known, leaving not only myself but also those who were listening, in awe of the knowledge given. By allowing ourselves to be inspired by the great philosophers and scholars of bygone times, who know where it could lead us.

Every-day in every-way, we are all being influenced by a force that we cannot see but we can feel or sense it. Often dismissing it has our imagination running wild, often through fear. Yes I was fearful when I started my spiritual journey into the unknown, but once I learned to accept it and ask for protection, my life changed. Bring all that I needed, when I need it, because they were the natural attributes of my higher consciousness. It allowed me the freedom to be able to pursue the different aspects and levels of my spiritual growth. The objective for me was to live my life as it was intended, by our Creator. In a blissful state and not being afraid to seek all that I desired. No longer, allowing my lower physical self to keep me in an unhappy state, all because I had disconnected from the source of my higher self and consciousness a long time ago.

When we have gained the ultimate Knowledge that leads to the infinite Wisdom, we then have to put our hard work into practice. In allowing ourselves to become our inner and true-self, the reconnection to the truth of our higher consciousness will set us free, naturally. But first, we must be able to recognise the illusions that we'd created for ourselves, all because of our unhappiness brought on by our lack of faith and belief in us. In the understanding of our disharmonious situations and the imbalances within, they can then be rectified, by elevating the problems or negativity. We must be able to know that by facing our negative emotions, we can turn them into positive learning's, and we'll have been use to responding to the negative emotions more often than not.

So instead of looking at life's learning's in the negative sense, we must only allow ourselves to look at the positive attributes of the lessons given. For example I was so use to looking at the negatives from the lessons given that one day I was given a sign that was meant in a positive way, and I took it as a negative learning. Not understanding the message given, until I took it on board as a positive learning I then learnt my lesson. Sometimes we can be very pessimistic not realising that we're self-doubting. When we can recognise the illusions within our lives, we would then only attract the positive lessons for our continued growth. We need to reprogram our minds and bodies into becoming more positive, allowing ourselves to experience our lessons, and then to understand the situations or circumstances given, but in a positive manner.

It is important that we allow our higher self and that of our higher consciousness to radiate from within into our outer world. It affects all that we do, but in a positive and successful way. We can then create balance and harmony in all that we desire and to what we can achieve. So, is the glass half full or half empty? The positive would be in saying it's half full, the negative would be to say, it's half-empty. In being optimistic you are being confident in the outcome, being of a positive mindset. So, we must only look for the good in everything that we see, say or do. In accepting all things that happen to us, we only then attract the positive learning's. It is about not buying into the fears or negativity of the different situations or circumstances that we may find ourselves in. Good comes from bad, but we have to look for it. We should take positive action to change the things that we do not want or like with our lives, and when we feel burdened, we should ask for help, and not struggle needlessly. When we are tried or weary we should know when to rest, and when we feel in doubt, we should do nothing accept allow us the opportunity to receive the information that's needed, before making a right decision. We cause us pain and grief by refusing to see everything in love, light and joy. We must give ourselves the chance to only see the positive attributes of any situation that we may find ourselves in. It enables us to release our negative undertones and fears of the lack of trust, faith, belief and acceptance that everything is, as it should be.

The journey of the soul can be quite an adventure; the secret is to acknowledge your own journey when the time becomes right, for you to do so. Until then, do not dismiss the evolutionary journey of the twenty-first century, because it is relevant to your continued spiritual growth. It is important to know that we need to be reconnected with the incredible gifts of our true selves and our positive attributes of all times. With the transition period of the physical self into this new age of rediscovery, our mystical gifts will help us to achieve all that we need, but naturally. We need to do this because of the changes that we've already experienced, and too the changes that are about to happen, and at times taking us all out of our comfort zones. With the present day challenges of our economic problems and the changes that we are being forced to make, will not be to our liking. A wake up call is required, so that we'll really see what is going on within every aspect of our daily lives. We are all worrying endlessly about the current state of affairs, wondering what will happen over the next few years. With a world recession and the uncertainty of our future, what can we do about it? To be able to connect fully to our true-self, would give us all what we need to survive, enabling us to reconnect with our positive accomplishments of

45

all times. But more importantly, to how we can take back the control of our true destiny and our everyday lives.

So remember everything happens for a reason, nothing is by chance. All we have to do is understand that if we buy into the negative mindset, it will only keep us in the lower conscious state of our needs and wants. We must appreciate all that we do have within our lives and not wait until something awful happens to a loved one or even to us, before we have a chance to make amends. To rejoice everyday in every-way, for all the gracious gifts that are bestowed upon us daily, will keep us healthy in mind, body and soul. To know that we do have choices, and that we do not have to put up with the various situations that causes us great distress. Just to be more accepting of our circumstances goes a long way in us coping with the situations that causes us to struggle with our lives.

The journey into the unknown does not have to be feared, it's a natural process, with the spiritual age of awakening will allow us to achieve our unrealised limitless potential. We must trust that all will be revealed when the time becomes right for us to know more. Until then, follow your life's pathway one step at a time, experiencing all that you can consciously. For life's adventures can take us into the mystical realms of our true selves and the unknown. Do not be afraid, just allow yourself to become who you have always been because by resisting this change will only create more pain and disharmonious situations for us to deal with in the long term. The external pressures cause us to move even further away from the power within us, and the lives that were intended. When we have successfully reconnected to our higher consciousness and the universal power of love, light and truth will reinstate unity and world peace.

CHAPTER 4

PATHWAY TO FREEDOM

What do we want freedom from? For most of the time, we are comfortable with our lives, but occasionally we will feel the unrest within. We long for freedom, from the restraints and restrictions that we have created for ourselves. Because we do not recognise or accept that what we have within our lives, is meant to be. When we cannot accept the different situations or circumstances that we find ourselves in, leaves us resenting certain aspects of lives. Which causes us to lose sight of what we are trying to achieve and in-fact do have, within our lives. We then find ourselves pursuing other interests because we have allowed ourselves to become disheartened or bored. This causes us to feel that life is not exciting anymore, leaving us struggling because we have lost the greater vision of what we want to accomplish.

Many of us follow self-improvement and spiritual pathways, in search of the miracle cure that would set us free. We travel the different pathways in pursue of other things that our pleasurable, experiences that make our lives so worthwhile. In acceptance, we would not place the restraints or restrictions that cause us to pursue other things, just to feel better about ourselves. This also causes us to take on too much, which then adds to the overall pressures that actually stops us from achieving the harmony and balance, in all that we do within our everyday lives; we automatically push ourselves to the absolute limits. This creates us to struggle and miss the opportunity of really enjoying all that we do have, within our lives. To understand freedom is to let go of the ego's demands and the prides no-defeat attitude, which creates our constant thoughts of our needs and wants, which causes the unrest within.

We all yearn for more free time, allowing us the opportunity to analyse the different aspects within our lives that we could then change, in order to feel better about ourselves. Freedom gives us independence, success, an inner peace and total acceptance, in all that we do. It allows us to be empowered by our personal truth of our intended lifetime, where our thoughts, actions and interactions with others, would become very rewarding. This gives us back the control of our true destiny and allows us to be fully in our lives and not just simply doing things within them, just to get by. Freedom requires commitment to the self, and our performance in successfully reaching our full potential will have us showing gratitude for all that we have accomplished. To understand freedom, we have to experience and practice nonattachment, to all things within our lives. This is about not attaching ourselves to the different things for security or a Well Being state.

The more we appreciate the simple pleasures of life, the less we rely on our needs and want. We then automatically go with the flow of life, as apposed too going against life. The pathway to freedom is of letting go of the things that do not serve us well, in other words, the things that do not fulfil or bring us complete happiness. Justification of our thoughts or actions is an indication that in what we pursue is not about our true intentions or desires. Trying to convince the self into believing that our thoughts or actions were with the right intention only brings us despair. Each individual has a responsibility to them, to become their truth at all times, and with all the different aspects within their lives.

My pathway to freedom was very arduous, at times being so frustrated that procrastination was a daily occurrence. I allowed myself to become a prisoner to my negative tendencies of the disharmonious situations within. With constant analyses of my thoughts and actions, was becoming so time consuming that it totally absorbed my life and energy, sometimes not seeing the wood, for the trees. It is about having the knowledge to know what we can change and the wisdom, to know what we cannot. To be accepting of all aspects and of the different situations within our life. This gives us the freedom to choose the things that we can change and when to change them. We must not be in a hurry to get rid of the not so nice things within are lives, because all the different situations and circumstances, have valuable lessons for us to learn? To off load to soon, could result in us being given the same situations or circumstances again, if we had not fully understood the implications of our thoughts or actions.

Everything happens in order for us to learn and understand from, so that we can move onto greater things. If we choose not to learn, we are basically saying that all is well within our lives and that we like things as they are. Our vulnerability will denote what is going on within; our attitude to how we perceive life's lessons is just another indication of our emotional imbalances or disharmony within. Our accountability of the events that have happened to us will play an important part in allowing us to successfully tread the pathway to freedom.

We all aspire and would love an idyllic lifestyle, with us achieving wealth, health and happiness within every aspect of our lives, but it takes a certain amount of luck. Success does not necessarily come from hard work, but from foresight and planning. We start off with good intentions, only to find that we have strayed from the vision of what we want to accomplish. We need to stay focused and unfazed by the different situations that block us, from time to time. We sometimes find that we have given up, due to things not working out as we had hoped for. We have to believe that we can accomplish our goals, even when the odds are against us. When we follow our dreams or our heart's desire it will bring us happiness and contentment, in all that we do.

The many pathways that we follow will eventually bring us to the pathway that will set us free. But first, we have to address and understand our important lessons, of our life's purpose. When we have successfully accomplished our learning's we can then pursue our dreams, knowing that we are actually on our pathway to freedom. We must be able to recognise our truth in all things, only then pursuing our dreams if we are completely ready for them to happen. If we are in any doubt or fearful in anyway, we will only block ourselves from achieving our goals. Our dreams being just around the corner, and we often feel frustrated because they're just out of reach.

When I was trying to achieve my goals I would put lots of effort in, only to find that I could not quite achieve them. It's so easy to throw the towel in, but with the determination to succeed; I would set about trying to understand the blocks, then to elevate the difficulties, and at times just to accept our demise, the blocks can fade away. In having the resolve to see a task through to completion, with clarity and focus, enables us to accomplish our goals more quickly. We need to recognise our problems, because in not doing so, just adds to the overall setback of thinking we have failed in some-way.

We need a constant connection to our higher consciousness that would then keep us in touch, with the greater understanding of our higher self and that of our truth or purpose. Only then, would we be able to achieve all that we had dreamed of. If we are rendered vulnerable, we are then unable to push forward because we are tried or depressed that life is not flowing properly. We then take the risk of becoming disheartened or disillusioned with our lives. We have to have an inner strength that would allow us to pick ourselves up and try again. All being a big part of our life's purpose and learning's of No Pain, No Gain.

So what sorts of things do we do, that takes our freedom away? We often find ourselves taking on far too much responsibility, telling us, we have to do this, that or the other.

All because of our expectations, family commitments or work pressures, we just seem to fall into the habit of thinking ourselves as indispensable. We sometimes kid ourselves that what we are doing, no-one else can do, often just allowing the natural roles in life to become your responsibility. They say if you want something doing, give it to a busy person and it will get done. Hard work never killed anyone, but what does is our perception which creates the stress and tension, we allow what happens to us through neglect of not knowing when to work and when to rest.

Our emotional imbalances or even the pride and ego, will keep us locked into particular mindsets that creates us to push ourselves too hard. The way we perceive the different situations within our lives, will keep us locked into the poor me syndrome. By feeling hard done too will make us feel unloved or not deserving in some-way, with the concept that we're being punished. We beat ourselves up, when at first we don't reach or realise our full potential, dreams or goals. To achieve freedom we need to realise that we are the most important person in our lives and by giving to ourselves first, allows us to give to others successfully. To elevate the disharmonious situations from within our lives, will allow us to become totally accepting of all aspects of our life. This enables us to take back control and encourages us to naturally go with the flow of life; receiving everything that we need, in which to accomplish our dreams or goals.

When the time becomes right we will achieve what we desire, but in the mean time we have to keep working towards our visions or goals. Once we can fully accept responsibility for our actions and thoughts, our higher consciousness will continue to encourage us onwards. Allowing us to be in a privileged position of being connected to the higher wisdom, will allow us our unique pathway to succeed and maintain a proper connection to the higher self and of all things. In achieving freedom of our thoughts, the restraints and restrictions would just disappear, allowing life to become much more exciting and very rewarding. We would then start to experience new adventures; life would begin to challenge us once more, but more importantly we would live the life that was intended. In recognising the coincidences and the incredible synchronicities of life, allows us to be in control of achieving our true destiny. To be living our life to the full, yet effortlessly going about our daily life, will attract only the positive attributes that are associated with what we are doing.

Freedom comes from realising our full potential, recognising who we've now become and to what we have accomplished. When we allow our true self to shine forth in all that we do, would truly be a revelation in understanding how powerful we have now become. This would allow us to pursue our dreams in earnest, pushing ourselves to achieve even greater things, treading into new territory. The more we can expand our energies and vibration, the more we expose ourselves too. The higher the vibration, the more established we feel, becoming empowered by our intuitive thoughts. Our actions would then bring spontaneity into a life that just flows. Once we have successfully released or surrendered our emotional insecurities and fears, associated with the constant battles of survival. We would truly be living our lives to the full, showing our appreciation of all things that we now have within our lives and of how the universe, has looked after us.

All that we need in life is provided for; all we need to do is just to wait on the will of heaven. When the time becomes right, all will be revealed, so what is revealed? The truth as to why certain things have happened to us and the real reasons behind our thoughts or actions. In understanding the reasons behind those learning's will help us to know what is expected from us. If we could just allow ourselves to be accepting of what has happened, believing that there is a more in-depth reason behind it. Because, we do not always need to know the reason as to why, just to be aware that there is a reason and to become more accepting of them. Looking for the positive attributes to any given situation or circumstances that we find ourselves in, creates a sense of Well Being.

The golden rule to treading the pathway to freedom is in acceptance, trust, faith and belief in you. Knowing that what's happened to you, you had pre-agreed before you came into this earthly life, and therefore was meant to happen. That being the case, you would also have pre-agreed to the solutions and the overall outcome of the different situations or circumstances within your life. Stored deep within your sub-conscious, and waiting for you to reconnect with, will give you access to all that you need, but when you need it.

Upon the learning's of our lessons there is no way we would have pre-agreed to an unhappy life. We are only unhappy because we have strayed from the source of the truth that is within. If we knew the truth, we could then accept what has happened to us graciously, because we would have understood the real reasons as to why we pre-agreed to the arrangements of our agreement, in the first place. So in acceptance comes trust in the outcome and faith in your own abilities that everything will be okay.

The rewards of living a successful life would also have been pre-agreed. So once we have overcome our life's purpose, we could then achieve our full potential, of enjoying our accomplishments in peace and harmony, with our soul-mate by our sides. But most of all, to be healthy in mind, body and soul, so that we can enjoy the simple pleasures that life brings, with contentment and peace that allows you to live-out the rest of your days in love, light and truth. When we reconnect to our higher self and consciousness, would we only then know true happiness? We always aspire to great things, which bring us abundance in all that we do.

Our true destiny brings our dreams into reality, allowing us to achieve the ultimate state of enlightenment. This allows you to reach your limitless potential, bring a state of balance and harmony within every aspect of your life. When this happens, you would know that you had achieved and was successfully living your life, to the full. This grants us freedom to manifest all that we desired and dreamed of, living our lives in peace and harmony, achieving Unity. To enjoy the freedom that comes from living your life successfully, allows us to live in perfect synchronicity and all lifetimes, becoming into one. This is the pathway of freedom, no longer being in pursuit of the soul's quest.

To allow yourself to become self and spiritually aware, unleashes your limitless potential to achieving your dreams or goals. The memories of which are stored within your sub-conscious. With the new Age of Aquarius allows the cleansing and purification of the sub-conscious and conscious mind. Which releases the memories of long ago to enable us to achieve all that we desire?

The pathway to freedom is the higher conscious mind influencing all that we do, say or think. It allows us to achieve our dreams naturally and when it is time for us to do so. We all evolve at different levels of consciousness, achieving the freedom to choose what rightful action will allow us to fulfil our obligation to the higher self and achieve our life's purpose, naturally. By not feeling threatened by what happens outwardly and of the things we have no control over, gives us acceptance, freedom automatically follows; knowing that what is not achieved to-day can be pursued tomorrow, keeping a clear vision of what we want to achieve.

If we do not hold onto the situations or circumstances that does not serve us well, will allow us the opportunities to seek new adventures and to experience life to the full. All of which is a part of our life's purpose and the pathways that we must follow, in order to realise our dreams. We allow ourselves to get stuck in the ruts of life because of the responsibilities that we hold ourselves too. This is because of our commitments to maintaining our life-styles when we are in-fact; all yearning for easier and better times. Fate sometimes steps in, forcing our hand into making life changing decisions. Maybe our lives being thrown into chaos in order for us to set ourselves free, from the restraints and restriction that we have allowed to happen to us out of necessity.

We are often afraid to allow ourselves to try new pastures, feeling vulnerable and threatened by change. Fate often takes a hand when life demands for us to be taken out of our comfort zones, so that we can grow and learn more about its divine plan. The Age of Aquarius requires us all to prepare ourselves for the spiritual transformation of our world. But more importantly ourselves, where we will we experience changes to the way we live our lives and to how we can cope with our true-selves and that of our truth.

With the realisation of other lifetimes we can accept that we have experienced death, many times. Our life's purpose is to experience freedom that at times only death as allowed us. Our life's purpose is to live our lives freely and successfully from the restraints we hold ourselves too. Death gives us that freedom but our lives are no more that's why we are reborn again in order to experience that freedom, whilst living an earthly life. With the constant battles associated with what we consider to be necessity, we end up giving our power of freedom away.

We all hypothetically travel the universe and back again, in pursuit of the freedom we crave. Trying to achieve peace and harmony within is an impossible task, when we had not even realised our disconnection from the source in the first place. To achieve balance between all things gives us the opportunity to realise that we hold the key to our demises. The reconnection to our ultimate truth of all things is the pathway to freedom that would allow us to live our lives in perfect harmony, and with all aspects within our lives reinstated, we would be living our dreams successfully.

CHAPTER 5

PARALLEL LIVES

We are all just a small fragmentation of who we truly are, and we're recycled souls travelling through space and time, trying to reconnect with the true essence of our ancestors, and that of our higher consciousness that holds the important details of our true selves. This information is stored within our collective consciousness until we're ready to receive or access the knowledge and wisdom of all lifetimes; this is our Akasha records and the Esoteric knowledge. We have to wait for the time to become right, in order for us to be able to comprehend what this important information is all about. It will enable us to be accepting all things within our lives, and helps us to live in the NOW!

By being accepting of all things will eventually lead us to the truth being revealed and understood, enabling our reconnection with the truth about who we really are, and to what we've can achieved within this lifetime. We need to be living our lives to the full in order to allow the positive and negative influences from previous lives to influence us. This gives us the opportunity to understand and realise the effects of all that we do, say or think whether in this life or other past lives. When we realise the importance of the negative undertones of our actions, will help us realise the potential of the important events that will happen to us, giving us a positive mindset to overcome our problems or issues. Once we realise why these things have happened to us, our lives would then be greatly influenced by the positive vibrations of all our accomplishments. But first, we need to realise that what is happening to us, was meant to happen and is an important part in who we really are, and to what we have pre-agreed to overcome or achieve.

When we eventually understand our problems, we will realise that our negative emotions or traits, was in-fact our lower consciousness or that of the pride and ego, keeping us locked into certain situations. With our constant thoughts and feelings being influenced by our higher conscious self, helps us to turn the negative situations within our lives, into positive learning's. This gives us the opportunity to access our pre-destined agreement to the events that would unfold within our lifetime, and tell the story of our true selves from long ago.

When all is revealed, we would appreciate the intricate workings of life's tapestry and the uniqueness of our true selves. We would realise that the negative undertones of our actions, was influenced by the positive vibrations of our truth, influencing us, in attaining a greater understanding of what our lives are all about. This allows the knowledge and wisdom to alter our state of consciousness, which grants us access to the infinite knowledge and wisdom of our positive attributes, of all times? Helping us to achieve the ultimate state of awareness, as our levels of consciousness expands, attaining the higher vibrations that will connect us to the collective consciousness of mankind.

Parallel lives are about the lifetimes that we have already had, but are parallel to this lifetime. Granting us with our greater understanding of what this life is all about. They are parallel to this one, because there will be similarities in the lessons that we must learn. But first, we must be in a similar mindset of the emotional insecurities or issues that we have to experience as part of our life's path. We need to take into consideration the different situations and circumstances, the different roles that we play and events that will teach us about our emotional imbalances and the disharmonious ailments within, In-fact, being part of what we did not fully understand properly in previous lifetimes, but are now created for us, within this life.

Our lives are about the important lessons that we didn't comprehend or perceived correctly in other lives, and they affected our lives enormously, which caused the unrest of our soul. All because, we didn't realise the consequence of our actions and to the imbalances that we created within. By not fully understanding the learning's at that particular time, will keep us struggling with our lives and to the different sequence of events that we must experience as part of our life's pathway. Our perception to the situations or circumstances and to how we have deal with them, will tell us a lot about our learning's or to the insecurities that we feel or have found ourselves to be in. Our vibrations influence this lifetime, with the emotional traits that attracts all that we need within our lives, in order for us to learn from. They are held within our energy field and the collective consciousness of humankind, helping us achieve the understandings of our life's purpose, which allows us to live a life, worthy of living. Once we are reconnected to our true essence of all that we have ever been, and to whom we have now become. Our soul would connect to the higher vibration that connects us with the life force energy of the Divine, Universal and Cosmic energies of the multi-dimensional parallels of all that is.

When time began, we were all innocent in mind, body and spirit. We were pure souls, with no preconceived perception of what life was all about. We experienced life in its true glory, trusting our instinctive reactions to lead us away from danger or situations that were not beneficial to our Well Being. As we continue to evolve our emotional state will denote whether we responded to the different situations in a negative or positive way. But as pure souls, we would only respond in a positive way. We would sense danger, taking the necessary precautions of self-preservation in order to keep ourselves safe and well. In a positive sense we would only act with pure intention, because we would not have been influenced by any of the negative emotional traits or the acts of a sinful nature.

As pure souls, we would not have been exposed or even experienced; the many unpleasant aspects of life that creates the emotional insecurities that are derived from living a life, on earth. But as we experience life, we would then become a product of the Cause and Effect of our thoughts, actions and decisions, taking the emotional imbalance and storing it within. The more lives that we have lived; the more negativity we expose ourselves too, which then adds to the disharmony. We are also influenced by each other, the different circumstances and the choices that we make. Life's experiences take their toll on the physical body, the mental pressure of trying to understand our problems or purpose. The undertaking of a life among the many incarnate souls, all of whom have a life's purpose to unfold with the influences of the many trials and tribulations of life, helping us overcome our lessons.

The importance of the knowledge that comes from acknowledgement of Parallel Lives is purely with the intention of us living our lives to the full. This allows us to become healthy in mind, body and soul once more, allowing us to act upon the knowledge given that helps us attain the infinite wisdom. The positive vibrations of all our existences from our time spent on earth, continues to influence our lives. Which allows us to attain a wealth of abundance within our chosen lifestyle, where we would be able to achieve a positive attitude to all things? This would then allow us instinctively to access our natural gifts, skills, talents and abilities, with us achieving creativity in all that we do.

Our Parallel Lives affect us in many ways; they form parts of our characters. The inherited characteristics of our personalities, our unique abilities, skills and the different aspects of our genetic identification that makes us all individual, in every aspect our lives. So, have you ever stopped to wonder who you may have been, in another incarnation? What you looked like, were you male or female or were you successful or poor? In which country did you live or the work did you did? And so on. We will all have been either gender at some time or other, experiencing all walks of life, in all of the different roles of mother, father, brother, sister and so on, even down to the different positions in life. We would have had role reversal, so what we did to others, we will have done to us, good or bad, in any possible scenario to any given situation. The synopsis of life is in the understanding of life's synchronicities, nothing is by chance, it's all part of life's great adventures allowing us to achieve our life's purpose. To attain the pure state of consciousness from the higher vibration that derives from the life that was intended for us to live. Instead of the life that we've created for ourselves, all brought on by our higher expectations of material gain, power and money.

We came into this life with nothing and we will leave with nothing, except the vibration of our soul, so think about what this means. What did we have that very first time we came to earth? We had an unblemished character, no flaws to our minds, body or soul. We were pure has God intended for us to be. But through living a life or the many lives that we have had since time began, we have ended up by deceiving ourselves. We have allowed ourselves to stray from the source of great intentions, but also from the life force energy and the life that God intended for us to have. The more that we have allowed the soul and ourselves to be deceived, the more negativity we have allowed into our minds and body, affecting our everyday lives.

Our state of unhappiness is created by our own expectations which results in frustration and procrastination, all because things did not turn out, as we had hoped for. The illusions of which create the imbalances or disharmony within our physical, emotional, mental and spiritual state. Which alters our level of awareness from what we think is real, instead of what is really real. The more that we travel away from the source, the more we become fearful of ourselves and the unknown. Through fear comes the detachment of the higher self and consciousness. The soul is who we truly are, the vibration that travels through the light years of all incarnations, travelling through space and time and a crusader of victory.

The mythical story of Adam and Eve they were the creation of God put on earth, pure in every-way. They were pure that is, until they ate the forbidden fruit from the tree of knowledge. It's human nature, a desire to experience anything that's forbidden. God gave us the freedom of choice, so who took our freedom to choose away? We did, we allowed ourselves to become fearful and so we gave our power away, once we started to doubt ourselves. God gave us all that we needed to sustain a healthy existence, we were his creation, connecting us to all things, the universe, mother earth, nature, even interconnecting us to one another, the family of life. He intended for us to live in unity, peace and harmony, with all of our needs being provided for. So what happened? Fear of the unknown, all because we forgot to trust, to have belief and faith in us, and our abilities. We forgot the promise that we made to ourselves of respect, honour and loyalty, and of being true to ourselves at all times. We are meant to experience knowledge to understand the difference between right and wrong. We should live our lives with the intention of being pure in mind, body and soul.

So Adam and Eve lived their life, and did what they were meant too, experiencing right from wrong. Acceptance of what happens to us, as it was meant to happen. No ifs or buts, they could not change what they had pre-agreed to happened, but they could learn from how they perceived what happened to them. This process allows us to able to forgive ourselves or others for all our injustices. With the knowledge comes the wisdom to know the difference between good or bad, turning any experience that we considered bad, into a positive learning. So with the next incarnation that they had would enable them to gain a deeper understanding of the previous life, and so on. The deeper learning's over the centuries will help us to achieve the potential of becoming pure in mind, body, and soul once again, but first we have to put right, what we've got wrong. In the acceptance of all things, we could have saved us from the pain and grief that we'd created for us and others.

Over the centuries, the vibrations of our planet are greatly affected by the negative vibration of the people whom resides upon it. At present, the vibration of our planet is much depleted, due to the lack of world peace, human strife and suffering. Also, due to our greed of our needs and wants, this has a very damaging effect on our planet, creating the environmental issues that we have today. We have all been made aware of the dramatic changes that we need to make, changes that will not just affect us personally, but everyone and everything within our world and its structure. We need to alter not just our perceptions, but our actions of why we do, what we do. Mainly because of the unhappiness that derives from what we think we need or want, instead of what we have.

We already have so much within our lives, but we are always looking for more. We are never satisfied; always searching for what we think we need, mainly the things that feeds our pride and ego. All of which are a constant battle, not realising that everything that we truly need, is already within. We are all born with everything that we need, stored within our hearts and soul. Within us all is the knowledge and wisdom, the ability to self-heal the will to pursue our dreams, the belief and trust in us and the truth about our actions. But more importantly, the connection to the life force of Mother Nature, the Universe and beyond. Because of our outward pursuits of our needs and wants, as contributed to our disconnection from the source, which then creates hardship on every level of our Being? So we need to understand where and when the disconnection occurred and too why?

The theory of Parallel Lives will give us the in-sight into the information that's needed to enable us to reconnect with that source again. Helping us to understand the sequence of events and to why they've happened? When we have attained the knowledge it will help us to understand the situations that we find ourselves in. This will give us the wisdom to overcome the many obstacles that stunts our progress, from time to time. It's half the battle, when we acknowledge the possibility that there is a reason as to why these things are happening to us. Just to accept that there is a larger force at work, a vibrational force that over-rides all other preconceived thoughts or feelings, a force that demands attention. When we ignore this vibration, our minds and bodies begin to break down through additional trauma. All brought on, by our refusal or resistance to the higher conscious self that would enable us to maintain balance and harmony within every area of our lives. When we can accept the higher consciousness as being our true selves, we would then create an abundance of wealth, health and happiness, within our lives.

Past lives influence us in a number of different ways; we have the negative emotional traits within our aura's attracting the lessons to us. Allowing the different situations or circumstances to be played out, but waiting for the time to become right, in order for us to overcome the issues or problems. We need to recognise that if something important happened to us in a previous life, say at the age of 21 years, we would not overcome the situation in this lifetime, until 21 years plus. We need to be of a similar mindset, before we have to deal with the issue or even to become aware that something is amiss.

Timing is everything, the right time; it's not time yet, at the same time or even to think that time maybe running out. We do have choices, we can chose to ignore time or accept that it's now time to sort our problems out, in order to achieve better times. Either way, we will find the pathways to help us achieve what we need. So whether we acknowledge that our lives are influenced by parallel lifetimes or not, the important fact is, we can choose, but whatever the case, just allow yourself the opportunity to stay open minded. By closing us to the possibility that there is more to life, than what we can see or touch, can slow the process of achieving our dreams and desires.

When we embrace our past lifetimes, it will enable us to let go of our fears, and we will then be more accepting of what our past lives were all about. With each incarnation that we acknowledge, will give us more depth of character, and more in-sight into our soul's journey. We then become a higher vibration with us making our world a better place to live, by being more self and spiritually aware, which affects not just us, but others too, who are also in search of their own quest? When this happens it will allow our consciousness to expand which then allows us to be our higher conscious self once more, in order to fulfil our dreams or goals successfully.

We live in a vibrational world, where everything that we do affects not just our planet but others, and ourselves, in so many different ways. Our environmental issues have to be addressed with our constant demands, and ignorance to the knock on effect of our actions, and the consequence of are huge to our cost of living. This has resulted in us now being rationalized; being made to pay a high price, for our needs and wants. This creates a state of panic when we are restricted from going about our daily lives, all because we took our resources for granted.

Life is the same; we take it all for granted, which has contributed in us dismissing the finer details of life. The important information that would have saved us from the unhappiness that we have created for ourselves, through lack of thought and trust. If only we had realised earlier, for the consequence of which, would not be so daunting, making us feel as thou we have a mammoth task in front of us to overcome. The same applies to the details of our lives, if only we had understood sooner, we could have saved ourselves from a lot of anguish, pain and grief. We are all required to put our lives back on track, but how? The things outside of ourselves put added pressure onto the overall environmental issues that we currently have. To work purely on our mind, body and soul, detracts from the current environmental issues, raising our vibrations to a level where we can make a big difference to the current state of affairs. By not wanting things needlessly, just to fill our voids within or to make us feel better about our insecurities instead of addressing the imbalances or disharmony within our lives.

Parallel lives will allow us to work on the physical body and our emotional issues, in-fact everything that we do. When we understand how the mind influences the body and how the soul influences the mind, we can then understand how the mind, body and soul are interconnected. Past lives are the characteristics of the soul, interconnecting with the life force of our universe, which then influences right action and interaction between all levels of our existence?

We have everything we need, to create Well Being, the reservoir of which is deep within us the evolutionary energy of the Kundalini, our heightened state of awareness that leaves us in a blissful state of All Knowing. By locating the truth within, all will be revealed but only when we have overcome all that is required from us. We need to know the truth about all things, because this would give us back the power to be able to live our life, effortlessly, and to be able to repair the damage that we'd allowed to happen, bringing about the realignment of the mental (mind), physical (body), and spiritual (soul) bodies, back together. This enables us to work on the higher levels with realignment to the Astral, Etheric, Celestial, Ketheric, Universal, Cosmic, Ascension and Emersion. All of which brings completion of the soul and its quest.

On the next page I have listed my thoughts of the different levels of spiritual growth, and the understandings of the soul's evolutionary journey. It's important to understand the soul's journey at each level of enlightened growth, and the continuance of our learning's will allow us to reconnect with the collective consciousness of humankind once more.

Levels of Spiritual Growth

PHYSICAL:- I exist, beliefs, concepts, and illness, thought programming, disease, cause and effect

MENTAL:- I think, perception, feelings, actions, interactions, emotions, knowing, skills and abilities

SPIRITUAL:- I Feel, I sense, intuition, awareness, gifts, growth, nurture, knowledge and wisdom

ASTRAL:- I Love, I give, receive, acceptance, forgiveness, inspiring, truth, intention and commitment

ETHERIC:- Higher Self and Consciousness, revelation, peace, harmony, tranquillity and joy

CELESTIAL:- At one, reconnected to life force of the universe and cosmic energies

KETHERIC:- Divine Knowing, All Being, Enlightened, blissful, higher concepts and Unconditional Love

UNIVERSAL:- All Knowing, at one with God. Manifestation of all our dreams, Limitless Being

COSMIC:- Gods Will, pure consciousness and grace, infinity, whole and complete once more

ASCENSION:- Completion, re-birth, Light seeking light, Enlightenment and pure essence

EMERSION:- Souls journey of evolution, superior, Divinity and All Encompassing

To work with the concept of parallel lives, is being able to understand what aspects we'd got wrong within this lifetime then being given the opportunity to put them right. All because, we'd lost touch with our true-selves, needing the trappings of a materialistic world just to fill the voids within. We are bleeding our planet dry, through what we consider to be necessity. How did we all manage, before the high polluting industry manifested our present climate, pampering to our greater needs of high-class living, greed and power, in order to feel better about ourselves?

It's been predicted that it will all end, the resources running out, eventually creating the distinction of our planet as we know it. The only thing that we will have in plentiful supply will be the natural disasters. Taking us all out, slowly but surely, but it's the survival of the fittest, but what does that mean? Being fit will not save us from disaster, the only thing that saves us, is our connection to the life force energy, and our truth. But also, to have faith, belief and trust in ourselves, and our mystical gifts and abilities that no matter what happen, we would be able to cope.

To be connected to the truth and higher consciousness, would give us the ability to listen to the small voice within, which would lead us away from any danger. Do not buy into the elements of fear; because fear will not save you, it will just bring the negative situations on. So to be connected to our true-self and that of our truth, is not just for the chosen few, but for everyone, where we would be able to take back the control of our true destiny. Acceptance of what will be will be, because this life is not about the trappings of material wealth, but the trappings that come from being spiritually united with our true essence of the truth, unity, and peace restored. But most of all, the Higher Consciousness, the Universal and Cosmic energies, that connects us to the life force energy of our Creator that's within us all. This grants us with the infinite wisdom to be living the life that was intended, a successful and rewarding life?

When we are fully connected to the real us once again, would enhance every aspect of our lives. We would instinctively know the greater attributes of the real us.

Because the things that we consider being our weakness will in-fact is our strength, and our greatest ally. We are all human, with areas within our lives, where there is room for improvement and attention. To nurture the self aids growth, making us more compassionate and understanding. Which will allow us to become non-judgemental, to be accepting to all the different aspects within our lives and to the choices that we make? Knowing that we are all right, in what we do, we are only judged wrongly through the lack of humility and understanding. Because of our past lives, we are not aware of what we have accomplished, let alone what we have done. We will have experienced all aspects of living an earthly life, good or bad, so we must not judge others because we cannot be sure that we are so pure of mind, body or soul. Because of the disconnection from the important information that would have made us more understanding and compassionate, allowing us to be accepting of the lessons that we needed to learn or overcome.

The lessons that we need to learn derive from living a life of not being connected to our truth and the power of the universe and creator. To know the details of previous lives helps us to be more accepting of this lifetime, to understand why the different situations have happened to us. This makes all the anguish that we feel, easier to bear. When we can accept that we have had an event in a previous life that we did not comprehend. We can then deal with our self-sabotaging tendencies that we'd not been aware of, due to a past life emotional imbalance within the unrest of the soul. Which has created a lesson that needs to be rectified within this lifetime, allowing you to gain a deeper understanding of the root cause? We are all given the opportunities every-day, so that we can understand the predicaments that we find ourselves in. All brought on, through a lack of trust in our own abilities, not being able to see a way of solving our problems. Maybe sometimes thinking we had, only to find the problem had reoccurred.

We need to achieve a deeper understanding to our problems, so we are given similar situations, in order for us to redefine the root cause. To analyse the situations whilst trying to make sense of our dilemma, makes us more aware of what is in-fact going on. Looking too closely at the self is a painful process that is why we've allowed ourselves at times to become disconnected or distracted with us focusing on others instead of us. Not realising that we are feeding the pride and ego, by thinking that we are okay when we are clearly not. With the pride and ego firmly in place, we become biased by our perceptions of any given situation, maybe being unprepared to compromise our beliefs, actions or thoughts. To compromise ourselves is to accept that we maybe in the wrong or that our emotional insecurities are running wild, allowing the self to be deceived. We need to recognise that we are pre-programmed with the negative traits of our life's learning's, based upon lifetimes of every possible scenario's being played out, within the different aspects of our everyday lives. So what sort of things are we supposed to acknowledge? Not what has happened to us, but why they happened?

Our perception to any given lesson will denote how we received the learning's. We view most unpleasant situations in the negative sense; we think we are hard done to or why me? What have I done to deserve this or that? We think life or God, is against us. When we view these situations with a positive mindset, we stand more chance of working our problems out. To be accepting, we know that it was meant to happen to us, all because of a lesson that we needed to learn, a higher vibrational force at work influencing us on. We would then be in a stronger position to see the greater understanding of what goes around, comes around, what we give out, and is what we get back, hence the lesson in the first place.

So going back to the beginning of time when we were pure souls, through the process of evolution the more lives that we experienced, the more we've strayed away from the source, with the source being our higher conscious self who connects us to the life force energy of God. This has resulted in us losing touch with the importance of life, and the inner self. We then began the process of disconnection from the power within, resulting in the lack of self-love, respect, belief, trust and faith, within ourselves. Thus creating the negative imbalances within, no longer recognising our self-worth, abilities, gifts or skills, anymore. With low self-esteem and no-worth, we make life hard work for ourselves, we them start to become dissatisfied with our lives. We then end up, doing things for the wrong reasons, just focusing on the surface of the imbalances or disharmonies that are within. Allowing ourselves to be influenced by what we think is important, from what is really important. Interestingly, when something bad happens to us, we end up with regrets; we then make dramatic life changes, trying to improve our situations, only to fall into the same pitfalls again, albeit later within our lives.

To be wise after the event is easy, but to maintain the wisdom, is to know the difference. If we had only listened to that inner voice deep within, we would have saved ourselves time, pain and grief. So why did we choose to ignore that nagging doubt or thought? Sometimes we think that the inevitable would not happen to us. It's a constant battle between the head and the heart, one or the other ruling supreme, instead of us achieving a balance between the two. By not listening to the voice within, we would not have realised that it would lead us onto the right pathway, allowing us the opportunity of getting our lives, right back on track.

The pathways that we have chosen for ourselves, why would we choose them if they only brought us pain? Maybe choosing a hard life, if we could have had an easier life instead. We chose the life that we did because of the lessons that we needed to learn, as our insecurities, perfectly matching our issues or problems. So as with Adam and Eve, they thought they had got it wrong, be eating the forbidden fruit from the tree of knowledge, but who said it was forbidden? They were innocent; they did what they were meant to do, because for whatever reason that the biblical story was told, it was about their innocents, purity and the nourishment of life. In attaining the knowledge when experiencing life allows us to know the difference between right or wrong, for Adam and Eve had not experienced a life on earth before. Their representation of man and woman was the beginning of the family of life and to experience unconditional love, and to have faith, trust, belief in us, and the ability to live their lives has it was intended by our creator.

It's not about quantity of lives that we've had, but the quality of life; same applies within every aspect of our lives. To experience all aspects of life, living our life to the full, makes it all worth-while. It's better to have loved and lost, than never to have loved at all. If we do not allow ourselves to experience all aspects of life, we would never know what we were truly missing, and could have achieved. We all hold onto situations that do not serve our higher consciousness well. Holding on, because we have become fearful, did Adam and Eve become fearful because they ate the forbidden fruit from the tree of knowledge? No, they trusted God; they took responsibility for themselves, living a life with the resources that God had given and when the time became right, they returned back to the source, willingly.

With innocents there is no fear. So you can be assured they did what they were meant to do, because it was a new experience and a great adventure to be living a life on earth, the beginning of mankind. From that moment on, they too, would have pre-known the course of events that would happen to them that very first time on earth. But they did not consciously, only on the higher sub-conscious level. The cause and effect of all our actions and interactions, holds the repercussions of what might happen to us in the future. The secret is in total acceptance of who you are, surrendering your worries or issues to God.

We are all a part of the greater force of the universe and we're pure at heart, but it's the illusions of life that leads us away from that purity, no one really sets out to make life hard for themselves or others. It's just the situations that we have created for us over the many centuries and incarnations, which has resulted in our lack of trust, faith and belief in ourselves? So whether we have had just one life or one hundred lives, a lot will depend on what's happened to us, to what this life is all about.

You can be assured that we have had more positive lives, than we have had negative ones. The reason being is what would be the overall meaning to life, if God intended for us to suffer and to be unhappy? He did not; all of this is our own making. That's why we chose to come back, because we wanted to get it right. We are all searching for the time when life really was worth living, achieving great things. Somewhere deep within our soul, is the calling to take us back home. So by going within allows us to take back that control of what makes our lives, worth-while and worth-living. When we reconnect with the power of the almighty, our life would then become a testament of our accomplishments of all lifetimes and that of our truth.

We hypothetically travel the Universe and back again, in search of your truth, and once we have reconnected with the life force energy of our planet and universe, will serve us all well in this lifetime and all future lifetimes. The evolutionary journey into the twenty-first century has begun; it will take us to the next level of our existence on this planet. Life and death go hand in hand, evolving to the infinite level of awareness, the higher consciousness of the soul. It's a comforting thought to think that there is more to life, than the suffering and strife, all man-made; it can be changed, but not overnight. To explore into the unknown expands our minds energy, but more importantly it allows us to live the life, that was intended. So it's important to open our hearts, as well as our minds, to the universal energy that has sustained al life on this planet, since time began. Embracing all opportunities, for they are the small steps that lead us to the synchronicities and challenges in life that enables us to reach our full potential. We could then live our lives with the positive vibrations, skills, talents and abilities from all past lifetimes, successfully reinstated into this lifetime allowing us to become our limitless potential.

Positive vibrations are about making the right decisions, being open to the positive influences of our thoughts and actions. When we allow our higher consciousness to guide us successfully along our chosen pathway, we are then able to listen to the inner voice within, enabling us to act instinctively on the information given. With no self-doubts about ourselves or our actions, gives us our innate wisdom which makes us a wise explorer and counsellor.

This enables us to become more compassionate and understanding, giving us natural poise, grace and dignity. This allows us all to help others instinctively, trusting our intuitive nature. We will then project positive healing energies to everyone we know, being able to naturally send out our positive energy, to anyone in need. Yet we'll maintain balance within our own life, on every level of our existence, even when we're under pressure, and in extreme situations or circumstances. We will all at some time or other, experience the pain that's created through us resisting change within our lives. But it's important to maintain balance and courage, through the different transitional periods within our lives, all being part of our life's path.

When we have maintained balance and harmony, our creativity will be unleashed, allowing our creative side to excel in all areas of our life. We'll then be able to experience our skills and talents that we're not aware of. Suddenly, time will not be an issue; we'll have all the time in the world, enabling us to pursue this newfound state of awareness, to enjoy within the different aspects of our lives and our beautiful world. Parallel dimensions are greatly becoming a phenomenon in our present time, the past, present and future, all becoming into one. The most important time is now, and the secret to life is to become our higher consciousness, the higher vibration of our souls, all Knowing and all Accepting, but most of all our true self, and truth of all that is. We will evolve and reconnect to our higher vibration brings the wondrous gifts of all times, into reality, and our unique talents, skills and abilities of all our accomplishments, mastery of our true self and the positive attributes of the higher consciousness. To be living a life where more and more people, are travelling their own unique journeys of their soul quest. In order to claim back the only vibration that will allow us to live our lives, as it was intended.

We originally did not choose to live life in purgatory, with suffering and strife. We are only here to repair the damaged that has already been done, through the endless need to survive, with the negative imbalances being evident within our carbon footprints. The sooner we understand this unique phenomenon, the easier our lives will become. To be able to access our true records of other existences, will allow us the opportunities that will connect us to our collective consciousness, influencing all that we do. This has a tremendous impact on humankind, our earth and the universe, a force more powerful when collectively united. So whether we are an individual, an army or a company, with the positive projection of our beliefs we can achieve great things. Even as an individual when we have collectively united all past lifetimes into this present lifetime, we would be a force to be reckoned with. But remember we can only use this higher vibration of consciousness, for the highest good of all.

As we travel our evolutionary journey going from lifetime to lifetime, our collective consciousness expands with momentum. Within each lifetime, it would only be possible for us to access what we need, when we needed it. Because this vibrational force would be too powerful that it would not allow us to live a normal life, on earth. We must have the faith that all will be revealed when we need it and not when we want it.

Because the more collective consciousness that we gather or connect with, the higher our vibrations will vibrate. We are only able to cope with a small proportion of these parallel lives whilst sorting our imbalances out, for the vibration would be too powerful for us. We have to take it slowly to attain the infinite knowledge and wisdom, all being stored within for prosperity. Once we had completed the process of becoming whole once more, we would then be in a position to become a higher evolved human being. Achieving the status of being enlightened, granting us with the opportunities and challenges, so we can continue the souls journey and quest, of Enlightenment.

We have been travelling our journey of the soul's quest through many lifetimes, in search of the truth that would set us free. This is not the first lifetime that we have had, where we are becoming aware of the importance of spirituality or of the souls evolutionary journey. For most of us, it just feels like the first time. In my first book, I explained the level of consciousness that we have at our disposal. We are born with our level of consciousness already set, enabling us to travel the universe and back again in search of the knowledge and wisdom. All stored within the Esoteric knowledge and the Akasha records, of our personal growth, which is accessed by our higher consciousness. The ultimate truth of our true selves and to what we can accomplish.

Once we attain this knowledge, we can then increase our level of conscious awareness. So on a scale of one to ten, ten being the maximum, just say that we were born at level two of the conscious ladder, with the aim to learn our lessons, successfully understanding all that we had pre-agreed. This allows our conscious awareness to increase, the more we grow and learn the more our minds energy expands. Within all aspects of spirituality, there will be a level of conscious awareness, allowing us to push the boundaries of the self. Helping us achieve new levels of consciousness and of our unique selves. Eventually returning to the source of our life force, at a higher level, than when we came into this lifetime. This allows us to become a highly evolved soul and noble warrior, in pursuit of all that is.

We have archaeological excavations studying the ancient cultures of the past. Our parallel lives are the archaeological excavation of the soul, a study to learn about the past, not of objects, buildings or even cultures, but of the soul. Our ancient's souls have roamed our earth for centuries, accomplishing great works of art, music and architecture, having extraordinary gifts, talents and abilities. These souls could quite easily have been us, in other incarnate form.

We really do not know who we have been or to what we have accomplished. But with access to the Akasha records of our higher consciousness that has recorded this information for our highest good, allows us to reconnect with the vital details that would assist in our continued growth and freedom. The enormity of the possibilities of this phenomenon is an incredible in-sight into the soul's quest. The soul has just one purpose, to evolve through space and time giving us the opportunity to reinstate our true essence, the essence of our higher consciousness that would actively play a big part, in allowing us to achieve all that we desired naturally.

The evolutionary journey of the soul is to reconnect with the collective consciousness of our universe. To unit with the life force energy of our planet, connecting us with everything and everyone, who exists within its structure? Scientists are pursuing the big bang theory, trying to recreate how our planet was created, the only creation that they should recreate, is our own. Only by understanding our own consciousness can we reconnect to the power of divinity, and only then would we be able to understand all of creation. To reconnect with the power of our source, is the higher consciousness and the collective consciousness of humankind. This would enable us all to become All Knowing, but to be All Knowing, naturally. Not adding to the destruction of our planet, by pursuing theories that can only add to our environmental issues of great consequence. When we become our higher consciousness, we can then reconnect with the collective consciousness of our planet and universe; divinity is a source of the Universe, the infinite power of all Creation.

CHAPTER 6

THE HEARTS FULL POTENTIAL TO LOVE

We came into this lifetime with pure love within our hearts, and we were loved by everyone, our parents glowing with unconditional love, joy and pride, at our safe arrival. We are pampered with love and attention for most of our life. As small infants we experience unconditional love, trusting our instincts and emotions. Then depending on what happens to us and to what we had pre-agreed; we slowly begin to lose sight of the unconditional love that we felt within. We then start to look to others to love us, and to make us feel good about ourselves or even just to recognise our worth. Not realising that we've already started the process of becoming the person that we need to be, in order to overcome the lessons of the agreement that we pre-agreed, before we were born into this lifetime.

Our emotional issues have caused us distress from previous lifetimes, where the negative emotion became locked deep within our sub-conscious minds. These deep rooted imbalances become our life's purpose and lessons, along with the issues that we have created for us within this lifetime, through the lack of understanding of what our lives are all about. We then begin to start the process of self-doubting with us showing signs of disbelief, trust and faith in us, which eventually results in low self-love.

Over the years of struggles and strife, we end up disconnected from our true-selves and risk falling out of love with ourselves, due to the cause and effects, of our negative perception to the different events within our lives. All brought on by our own insecurities of why we think these things have happened to us, in the first place. We then project our fears outwards, sometimes projecting them onto others, our insecurities making hard work of what we want to accomplish or achieve, within our lives.

Over the centuries the greatest love songs have made our hearts swell with joy. All you need is love, says it all. So how can we achieve, the hearts full potential to love? Just stop and try to feel the love within, do we really know what it feels like? I just focus on my children and grandchildren to know what the feeling of LOVE really feels like; my heart just fills of love and blissful joy. But do I feel it for myself? There was a time that I did not, but the scary thing about it was that I didn't even know, when I'd fallen out of love with myself. All you need is love, because without it we become lonely and unhappy. I always knew I could count on the love of my family and friends to see me through the hard times, but the love within for me was not so evident. The realisation that we do not love us or even like ourselves at times causes us great concern and distress.

So my inner journey began, a slow process of elimination of my imbalances, forgiving myself for how I had perceived certain situations or circumstances within my life. Mainly out of a lack of trust in myself, and with the process of my inner journey I made a conscious effort to restore harmony and balance within, once more. Loving the self took a little bit longer, because I had issues and lessons to overcome that were an important part of my life's path, and it required in-depth understanding in order to overcome.

With the aid of the holistic techniques, culture and affirmations, the process of loving me began. Little by little, faith was restored within, and the belief that I was good enough, paid off. As soon as I started to say NO to the demands of others, put my needs first, it was not long before a balance between my needs and the needs of others, was achieved. I am the most important person in my life, because if that was not so, I would not be in a position to look after others. People think it's selfish to put our own needs first, but if we don't, who would? That is a sad fact, but please, do not learn the lesson the hard way, because it was a lesson that nearly destroyed me.

We have to love ourselves completely, with all our imperfections, so if we're okay with whom we are, so will others. There is too much emphasis on perfection, to what we should look like, wear and have within our lives. We are always living up to the expectations of what we expose ourselves too, making us more and more dissatisfied with who we really are. Depending on how bad our persistent cravings are, denotes how much we have travelled away from the source of self-love within.

To have wealth and all the trappings that go with it is great, as long as we do not substitute it, for love or our happiness. Our outer appearance should not mask the insecurities that we feel within. If we loved ourselves unconditionally, we would have everything we actually needed within our lives, to feel safe and secure. Not pursuing perfection within our outer world, in order to fill the voids, within. The only things that really matter, is our-self and our families, the love and great times that we all share together are priceless. The meaning to life is LOVE, the meaning of death, is the continuation of that love, for love is eternal.

When we allow our hearts its full potential to love, it's to love ourselves first, then others. This allows love within to flow outwards, enabling us to love all of nature and humankind, in fact all of creation. It is never too late to learn, it is never too late to say you're sorry, to forgive ourselves and others, for what we consider we've got wrong. All we need to do is get in touch once again, with the people who've played an important part in our lives? Maybe someone who taught you some valuable lessons in life or even a teacher who encouraged and believed in you, when others did not. Lost family members or loved ones, friends or acquaintances that we have not seen in years.

Do not wait until someone is ill or even on his or her deathbed, before you get in touch. The greatest gift to give you is to be open to love, to give love and to receive love. In communication we expose ourselves to the greater love, if we show love and compassion, it allows us to become tolerant and kind. When we put ourselves and others under pressure, we risk losing confidence in ourselves and to what we are trying to achieve. To allow everyone the space and time to excel, would allow us all to achieve great things, but at our own pace and time then we don't risk falling out of love with us or others.

Once we start caring deeply for those closest to us, we are then able to care for those who we do not know, but are suffering in some way. We are not always able to be with those we love, but it does not stop us from picking up the telephone or even writing a letter. This world needs more love, we all need more love and if someone we know does not love him or herself, then you should show them, your love. A smile or a gesture goes a long way. There was a time when I was so out of love with myself that I would not allow others in, but I know with their perseverance, I eventually was able to find my way back and to see myself through their eyes, and with love.

When I started to really look at myself, what I first saw was a sad person who'd forgotten to smile or even to laugh, someone who had fallen out of love with not just life, but themselves. Yet someone who really did care about what happens, but I had forgotten to rejoice in the things that really mattered. It was not about the material wealth that just offered comfort, from time to time; it was about the people that I really cared for. What I'd been searching for was love, sometimes thinking it was a love of another, only to find out it was the love of myself. Not just any old love, but to love myself completely and unconditionally. Because deep with my soul was such a love that held a shining light, a beacon of light that showed me the way home. Home is where the heart is, for love is all around us, and it radiates and illuminates into our world, and in all that we do, say and feel, for we are love.

When I started to laugh once more, it was a strange experience, because it was a deep laugh from somewhere deep within my soul. Realising that the laughter I had displayed in the past was half hearted, making me realise that a lot about me had slowly been dying. I was not aware of how unhappy I had become, pressing myself destruct button. Thankfully with divine intervention I was given a second chance, all because I had pre-agreed to get it right, this time around.

What had made me so unhappy was the lack of love for myself, realising that my unhappiness was just a state of mind. Created from my lack of faith, trust and belief in me, and my own abilities, others saw my worth, unfortunately I did not. Once I started to believe in myself again, I was well on the road to recovery. We don't actually lose the love for ourselves, we just project it into other areas of our lives, and my focus was mainly on my children and family. Realising that when I focused on my own ambitions and dreams, I'd not pursued them for the right reason that's why they didn't turn out has I'd expected them too. This caused me to become frustrated and disillusioned with life and me, which just added to the negative emotion of not liking me anymore.

So by the time I started my inner journey, I felt it was a mammoth task, would I ever be able to comprehend my lessons? When I first started to alleviate my imbalances from within, I had no clue to what they were all about. But through the process of elimination, I was always made aware of the lack of love that I felt within, for myself. On clearing the mind and body of the negative thought patterns, I slowly began to realise that I'd been happy; it's just that the challenges in life had made me focus on my unhappy times instead. Once I'd understood and released the imbalances which were my perception of how I had viewed the different events, within my life.

I then began to realise that I'd had some fantastic times, and the memories would carry me forwards. We all have periods within our lives where we seem to really struggle with ourselves, all because we have not recognised what in-fact, was going on within us. When we can accept ourselves with all our imperfections we'll feel really comfortable with whom we are, we then realise that we do love ourselves. For deep within our soul is just such a love an unconditional love that loves you back without a price tag. Otherwise I wouldn't have recognised the unconditional love as being the LOVE that I'd been searching for all of my life. For deep within us all, is the memory of a time when unconditional love was instinctive and pleasurable. It was love with no hidden agenda; it was a love that loved you back, no matter what. It was an unrequited love, a love that knows no boundaries, an insurmountable love.

When we love ourselves unconditionally, the love that we feel is whole. We are no longer searching to fulfil the imbalances within; so the love we then feel, is complete. So when we love a friend, family or partner the love we feel is in equal measures. The depth of that love is mirrored by the souls that we share our lives with. The infinite knowledge of the Esoteric and Akasha records holds the vibrations and the divinity of all souls who come together, and within any lifetime. We all react to the inner vibration of an infinite soul that connects with us, being graced by all that we share, within our lives.

With each incarnation and to whom we spend our lives with, will denote in the coming together of soul-mates. With all people that we meet within our lifetime, there will be some who we share our lives with, not in order to feel whole, but to complete a cycle of infinite love. The souls that we have an affinity with are the souls that we met and shared other lifetimes with. Some are just with us for a short duration, others being with us for life. But whatever the case, we will never be divided by death, for love lives on through each and every-one of us, stored within our hearts and memories, and it's an eternal love.

The journey of the soul only becomes complete when we've hypothetically travelled the universe and back again, in search of the truth that's within us. This allows us to successfully connect with our truth, which enables the love within, to set us free. But more importantly, the understanding of the infinite love, allows us to bask in all its glory. The meaning to life is love, the infinite ocean of a blissful Love. No other person can give you love, for you are love. Love is all around and within everything; it permeates all of life itself. When we give love or receive love, it's because we are love, because our whole being is open to the greater Love.

When all of our lessons have been learnt and understood, we can go forth to live-out the rest of our lives in peace and in-love. When living our life's to the full, we must keep love within our hearts and vision. See love, in everything that you do and everyone that you meet. Never look for the downsides of life, leave the negativities alone. Just focus on the opportunities and challenges that life presents to you, with love, joy and light. The positive attributes radiating outwards, for its shining light will keep the pathway to success, open. The pathway that will allow others to find what they are also searching for, in achieving the reconnection with the truth that allows them to be embraced by this infinite Love.

The Universal Law of Love; this is to love yourself, because until you love yourself no-one else can. We have to reconnect with our inner self on all levels, achieving our higher consciousness then being able to love all things, unconditionally. Unconditional love has no price tag; it loves you back no matter what, without any expectation of reward.

It's a love where your feelings never alter; you never feel challenged by others insecurities or decisions, being there for them. A powerful love that's unspoken and the recipient never questions it, to give unconditionally to other less fortunate than you.

This is a love that is attained once you have reconnected to your higher consciousness and the enlightened state of awareness. Enlightenment is the reconnection with the whole of creation, connecting us with the power of infinite love of all that is.

CHAPTER 7

DREAMS AND AMBITIONS

Even as small children, we would have had our dreams and ambitions. Often hearing ourselves say "when I grow up, I want to be a teacher, a fireman" and so on. For me, I wanted to be a nurse, a dream I'd had for a long time. Then one day, while working at the local Vets, (It was my Saturday job, while I was still at school). I watched then operate on a cow; I had never seen so much blood. Sadly, that put paid to my dream of wanting to be a nurse. I have always found myself, being drawn to helping others, even today; my life's purpose is about helping others to overcome their problems. So within each one of us, is the dream of pursuing careers that best suits our natural skills and abilities. This will allow us to excel in the different lifestyles that bring our creative talents, forwards into reality.

Dreams are the memories from long ago, of other lifetimes where we achieved all that we desired and we used our natural abilities, instinctively. We sometimes have our dreams for a long time, before we can pursue or even be able to achieve them. The realisation in understanding the abundance that comes from living our dreams. In other words our dreams are about fulfilling a desire to be successful, but naturally. But also to do the things that make us really happy and content, being at one with ourselves, in all that we do. For some, we chase our dreams but never seem able to bring them, into reality, why? Perhaps we want to accomplish our dreams for the wrong reasons. The moment we pursue our dreams in order to feel better about ourselves or even just to make ends meet, thinking it would change our lives by filling the void within. This is when our dreams are in danger of becoming a chore, the pleasure of living our dreams, is then taken away.

We have lots of dreams, but we must allow ourselves to continue one step at a time. Not being phased that the time may not be right, in which to pursue our dreams. That does not mean, our dreams will not materialise in the near future, but until they do, they will remain our ambitions or desires allowing us to work slowly towards achieving them, one step at a time. Sometimes we get very disheartened, while waiting for our dreams to come into fruition, not realising that we're in-fact already living part of our dream, so we need to take small achievable steps to achieving our dreams. It is important, never to lose sight of what we want to accomplish or achieve, keeping a clear vision of our goals. We often beat ourselves up from shear frustration or disappointment, causing us pain and grief. Through the lack of trust, belief and faith in ourselves, we risk losing sight of our dreams. We then allow our dreams to become a burden, the mundane things in life taking precedence.

We sometimes loose the greater vision of what we what to accomplished thinking that we cannot achieve them, because we have given priority to other things. Kidding ourselves that's it is through the lack of money, time or even self-effort. We all start off with good intentions, only to find ourselves going down other pathways that we really hadn't planned too. Time and money in short supply, putting our dreams off until another day. As with all things in life, there's plenty of time to pursue our dreams but when we're ready to do so. So by enjoying and living in the Now, helps us look for the positive attributes in all that we do and have. We would then; not need to worry needlessly, about what we feel is missing within our lives. If we allow us to appreciate the opportunities that life has already presented to us, knowing that it will continue to do so, this allows us to achieve all that we desire naturally, bringing our dreams and ambitions into reality.

There are times when we find ourselves doing things within our lives, not realising they were in-fact part of our dreams. When I was working in the company that I built with my first husband, I had a job that I loved. I found it to be very rewarding, enjoying the challenges and the responsibility, of organizing some of the buying and selling of the products, for the different outlets. But over the years and through the pressures within my personal life, I began to lose sight of what I'd once enjoyed. So consequently my job became a chore, I no longer enjoyed the work I did.

After divorcing my husband and my job, and when I started to pick the pieces up after the breakup of my marriage, I found I really missed my job, but it was too late to change what had happened. I missed the challenges and the working together as a team, but more importantly it was the job I missed the most, it had allowed me to use a lot of my natural skills and abilities. So with all things in life and because of the outside pressures, we risk giving up on things that we loved, not realising what we'd had, until we haven't got it anymore. The moral to the story is, to really appreciate all that we do have within our lives and to what we've accomplished, but more importantly, to enjoy every aspect of lives while we still have the time too. I have always treasured my family that really was never an issue it was myself that was the problem!

The journey that followed I did not have faith and totally believe in myself anymore that I ended up pushing other dreams away. Maybe putting things on hold until I felt better about myself, and at times watching others achieve their dreams, thinking that it only happens to them, that it was never my turn. I did not realise that I had a negative mindset, feeling hard done too, thinking I was being punished in some-way for a crime I hadn't committed. But the truth was, because I felt hurt and disillusioned I did not believe in myself anymore, to actually allow myself to pursue other dreams. All because my mindset was, I'd worked hard for twenty five years within the company that we'd built together, and I hadn't got the

89

resolve or confidence within me, to do the hard work or the sacrifices, all over again.

Over a period of time, life demanded that I should be taken out of my comfort zone and presented me, with the opportunities that once recognised, allowed me to pursue other interests that enabled me to realise my potential. With the realisation that I'd focused on other people's lives and helped them to pursue their dreams, instead of my own. Even though I enjoyed my job within our company, there was another more important job that I was about to do that was even more rewarding. But my fears, and with the lack of understanding had allowed me not to recognise my truth, of my life's path.

Once I accepted the challenges, I realised the job that I was now doing, was like no other. It gave me an oneness within, and I felt really comfortable with myself, it was a job that came naturally to me and I loved. I was able to allow the universe to give me what I needed in order to carry out this work. We have to love ourselves enough to say no, to the demands of others and outside pressures, at a time when we need to propel our own dreams forwards. The sad fact is, no-one else can do this for us, so to break the cycle of unrealised potential is in recognising and believing in yourself, once more. This enables us to achieve our full potential, bring our dreams and ambitions into reality; this gives us the star role in the production of our life. To witness our life first and foremost, to make sure we have everything that we need to fulfil our agreement and dreams of our unrealised potential.

So our dreams and ambitions, is our unrealised potential of the real us, pushing us towards achieving all that we desire. Our higher consciousness is the soul within that speaks to us through our thoughts and feelings, encouraging us onwards. But first, we must be able to break ourselves free, from the chains of the restraints and restrictions that we hold ourselves too, and holding us back through fear or allowing the negative mindset to tell us that we do not deserve in some-way. This causes us to experience low self-esteem, no self-worth or even a lack of confidence. The negative traits of fear telling us that it's beyond our limitations, but with right intentions we can give ourselves the permission we need to succeed. Where there's a will, there's away. We can achieve anything that we want to achieve, as long as it's for the right reason.

When we do things for the right reasons they will grant us with a sense of peace and tranquillity within our lives, enabling us to express our creativity in all that we do. This would allow us to be able to explore new boundaries of our inner self and within our outer world, bringing pleasure not just to us, but also to others. We would then be able to leave behind after our deaths, a legacy of the vibration of our truth for future generations to benefit from. The vibrational blue print of our true-selves is stored within the collective memory of all that is, and for us to recall sometime in the future, just in case, we pass by this way again, another life, in another century. Remember, nothings by chance, everything happens for a reason.

Do you ever stop to think about child geniuses, people who have artistic qualities or play a musical instrument? Yet they had never read a musical note or even taken an art class, but from an early age they have displayed or produced incredible mater-pieces. We are all born with abilities, maybe not of a genius nature. But who is to say that later on within our lives, we may be able to achieve such accomplishments. We would only accomplish them, once we've reconnected to our higher consciousness, and have overcome the lessons in life that we'd pre-agreed too, and reconnected with our limitless potential. Some of us, have experienced some pretty dismal times, maybe traumatic situations that we felt we'd never recover from them, only to find that in time we have, allowing ourselves to move onto better times. When we've overcome all that is required from us and having understood our lessons, we then gain a deeper understanding into our life's purpose. This enables us to experience the creative abilities that we'd only dreamed of.

When we have reconnected to the higher consciousness, we can then decide if we want to travel the pathway of enlightenment, and activate our genius gifts or abilities. Some people are born with their dreams and unique gifts already in place; others have to work hard to achieve them. But whatever the case, we are all doing exactly what we're supposed to be doing, everything that we'd pre-agreed. The gifts, talents and abilities are already within, just waiting for the time to become right, to access them; we must allow us to perfect these gifts and abilities, to the highest good of all.

We do not give ourselves enough credit; we undermine our own abilities. Sometimes allowing others to put us down or even to believe we are wrong in some-way, in what we're doing. Accepting our lower physical self, enables us to cross the bridge to the higher physical, mental and spiritual self, which reinstates the power of intention and action. This power connects us to the universal energies, allowing us access to our collective memory of actual accomplishments of this life and others. The vibration of our dreams allows the higher consciousness to bring them into reality, granting us with our desires and dreams naturally in order to become successful.

I held myself back from accomplishing my dreams, through the lack of money and belief in myself. Often focusing on others, always putting my dreams off until tomorrow, only tomorrow never came. Why would I do this? Every-day I would make some sort of effort, a bit like two steps forward then three steps back. What I did not realise was that I was making an effort, but until I understood the illusions that I'd created for myself, I would not be in a position to propel myself forwards, in earnest. I really had to say no to the outside influences, loving myself enough to give myself permission to pursue my dreams first and foremost.

I was then able to close the doors on the situations that were not about my highest good. I was fearful of making any decisions and getting it wrong. How many times had I gone down a particular pathway to find that things had not worked out, the way I had hoped for? So my negative mindset kept me in a comfort zone where I was not feeling challenged anymore. I just went along with the different situations within my life, waiting for some divine order, to show me what to do next. Honestly, how could I have been so blind? We all at some time or other, only make half-hearted attempts in pursuing the things that we feel are important to us. Kidding ourselves that what we are doing, is what we consider to be our best efforts. So a big wake-up call was required! For me it was having written my first book and sending it to the publishers, the process seemed to take forever, I didn't realise that deep within me was a fear, a fear of moving forwards, and a lack of confidence and belief that I could succeed.

So, due to fear, I was on an unconscious level preventing my book from being published. It was about me moving forward, but in order to do so; I needed to close certain doors on the parts of my life that had been a traumatic or a distraction. The beliefs and concepts that had been distracting me from getting on with what I really wanted to pursue, and accomplish. All because of my fear base of will I fail is I good enough or will I really achieve my dreams and desires before time runs out. It was a fear derived from years of frustrations, and the rejection of my ideas. So now I had to give myself permission to succeed and moved forwards in earnest. We must all realise that by achieving our dreams or goals allows us to grow and learn more about who we truly are. When we unleash our true selves we will realised our full potential, allowing us to become a limitless Being.

To be successfully living out my dreams, I needed to recognise what my dreams were, and why I wanted to pursue them? So I needed to consider what would make me really happy? I was no longer sure of. Realising that my belief was that my happiness was in the hands of someone or something else and I felt like I'd been waiting all of my life to pursue my dreams, but what are my dreams? My dreams are, to be living my life to the full and to the best of my ability, also in achieving things naturally, giving me contentment and fulfilment in all I do.

To have a vocation that challenges me was important, but also would bring great satisfaction, not only helping myself to achieve, but also others. So I became a self awareness mentor which enabled me to share the knowledge and wisdom, with enthusiasm and passion that comes from being connected to the higher self. This helped me to enjoy my life to the full, experiencing the new adventures and challenges within my life, whole heartedly. The most important dream is to be fully in my life, and not simply doing things within it, just to pay the bills. But most of all to be healthy, happy and content in all that I do. I enjoyed the communication and interaction with all aspects of humankind, nature and the universe, bringing Unity, Peace and Harmony.

I use to dream about being rich, being important and to experience wealth with all its trappings, often focusing on the things that were constantly put before my eyes, pursuing other people's dreams or lifestyles, thinking it would also make me happy. I did at one time, have a privileged lifestyle, but I left it all behind to find true happiness, but this happiness only comes from within, when you have successfully understood your life's purpose or lessons, and have overcome all that you'd pre-agreed. This will enable us all to set ourselves free to follow our heart's desire, being able to bring all that we have ever dreamed about, into reality. But most of all, to be able to say that I do a job I absolutely adore, and brings me great satisfaction. This would allow us all to perfect our unique abilities, whilst exploring the deeper depths within our soul. The realisation that we're already living our dream, by helping others who are also on their own pathway to self-discovery of their authentic self, brings great satisfaction.

Once we have reawakened to our dreams, we will realise the potential of the journey of reconnecting with our true essence of the real us, and the higher consciousness of our higher self, where the memories of our dreams that we achieved long ago are stored, and accessed. When we are truly ready and the time becomes right, we will realise that our dreams have already come into fruition, achieving what we have always desired and inspired too. The vibration of all that we'd accomplished, and has been recorded for prosperity, with the memories of which, keeps our dreams alive. So when we're ready and the time becomes right for us, we will all reawaken to the truth that we are being true to ourselves and that we're keeping the promises that we made?

As we travel through life, experiencing and enjoying all that we pursue, enables us to understand the truth that sets us free. When we know of the real reasons behind our thoughts, actions and to whom we truly are, aids in the realisation of achieving our full potential, and becoming a limitless Being. The soul's quest is to live our lives effortlessly, but with the sole purpose and intention of fulfilling our dreams, naturally.

We need to recognise and follow our natural paths, in life. The more confident we are, and the more established we feel, with all that we have within our lives. With the right attitude and balance between all aspects of our lives, grants us with a strong connection to our dreams and goals. We must be able to move on through the different transitions within our daily lives, without feeling threaten or insecure. But allow ourselves to take in, new ideas and allow our lives, to change naturally. To have the strength and allow our wisdom to lead us forwards, will propel us into this new century of great intention, being excited and enthusiastic about all aspects of our lives, whilst pursuing our dreams. Knowing that we're not given anything that we can't cope with, for all is pre-agreed.

The Golden Age of Aquarius is upon us, and with a strong connection to the earth and universal energies, will sustain all future growth, allowing us to achieve all that we desire naturally. The future holds great things for us all, but first we must let go of all suppressed negative emotions within the conscious and sub-conscious minds. This will allow us to face our futures with renewed confidence, having total faith, trust and belief, in all that we pursue. We must have the courage to face the uncertainty of what the future holds, knowing we can overcome all that's required to live a successfully and rewarding life. Our dreams are the future; so just allow you the opportunity to bring them into reality, the past, present and future, all becoming into one.

CHAPTER 8

INFLUENCE OF OUR THOUGHTS

Our thoughts are very powerful, with some of our thoughts being our higher consciousness talking to us. The thoughts we have, play an important part in how we perceive what happens to us, and of how they influence the mind, body and soul. We all have knowing thoughts that guide us through life, enabling us to make the right choices or decisions. Our thoughts influence everything that we say or do, but we can control our thoughts, allowing ourselves to only have positive thoughts which then influence our actions. The negative thoughts are fed by our insecurities, self-doubting and self-sabotaging tendencies, and also our emotional states plays havoc with our state of mind, creating mental pressure or exhaustion. We have thoughts as the sub-conscious transmits signals from the mind, in order to influence our actions and the physical body. The illusions that we create for ourselves, influence the perception of the thoughts that we find ourselves having. A thought can be received in either a negative or positive way, depending on our state of minds. Often allowing us to become confused, not always being able to make our minds up about the situations or circumstances that we find ourselves in or to what we want to accomplish.

We need to be detached from the things that are going on around us, in order to act successfully on the thoughts received. There is a very thin line between the thoughts that we pre-think, to the thoughts that just come naturally into our minds. We cannot stop our thoughts as they instinctively give us the opportunity to contemplate our feelings, our ability to consider the consequence of our actions. To be thoughtful is to consider and to be responsible for our actions or outcome. To be thoughtless is to be inconsiderate, excepting no responsibility for our actions or there consequence. The influence of our thoughts can be very destructive if we do not understand their true meanings. Our minds influence the physical body, our gestures, posture and all ailments and illnesses. It also influences the attracter field around our physical body, a vibration that travels with us from lifetime to lifetime, attracting the lessons that we need in order to learn from. When we are in a negative mindset we attract the negative experiences from life, but the positive mindset only bring the positives into our lives. So we need to be very careful in what we think, because what we send out is what we get back. So let me explain some of my thoughts and their consequences.

When I was at low ebb, feeling the world was against me, I found it very difficult to pick myself up and get on with my life. Making a half-hearted attempt at achieving my dreams or goals, only to find things had not worked out the way I had expected them too. Being frustrated, I realised that my negative mindset had kept me from achieving my dreams or goals. In justifying my disappointment I thought that life was against me, I would blame others or the different situations for my demise. I had allowed myself to be influenced by the negative undertones of my thoughts and feelings. Through frustration, and with no faith or belief in myself, I had allowed myself to think that I was hard done too. With my thoughts confusing the issues, I'd allowed myself not to trust the self into making decisions anymore, afraid of making the wrong decision.

For a very long time I was not aware of my negative thought patterns. I would have a positive thought but I would sabotage them, by only making a half-hearted effort. Or I would have a negative thought and end up beating myself up, all because I thought I had got it wrong in some-way. We have the pride and ego playing a very big part in the confusion, creating the illusions within our lives. Through pride, we will not allow ourselves to own up, to what is really going on. The pride keeps us in a place where we constantly beat ourselves up, procrastinating from frustration, anger, disappointment and fear. Feeding the ego, deceiving ourselves into thinking we're okay when the truth is, we're not. This mindset creates the unrest of the soul and the ailments of the physical body, all being influenced by the pride and ego, creating the imbalance or disharmony within.

Thoughts can be very destructive, because we create for ourselves too much mental pressure, from trying to understand what we should be doing and to where we are going wrong. Often changing our minds because we could not make a firm decision based on what was going on within our lives, our thoughts being a constant battle. At times we're not able to sleep because of our thoughts or anxieties, keeping us awake. This is when we create stress and tension for ourselves, the number one killer.

Some of our thoughts are pre-programmed, with the information that we need to enable us to understand our life's purpose. We can re-program or re-educate ourselves at any time, achieving this by altering our perception of what we think our lives are all about. Also by not buying into the poor me syndrome, becoming a victim to your own negative belief system. For me this revelation came, once I had reconnected to my inner self and that of my truth. When we know why we are here in this earthly carnation, the solutions to our problems are easier to achieve and understand. So for me, to know that I had come to deprive myself, physically, emotionally, mentally and spiritually, was truly a revelation. With the mindset of thinking I'd got it wrong, to the realisation that I'd listened to my thoughts, and acted on the information given, in order to learn my lessons and life's purpose. This resulted in the actions that I'd taken, because if I didn't truly believe that the decisions that I made were the right ones, I would not be the person that I now know myself to be.

With all unpleasant experiences, we do what we have too, because it's about not putting up with anything that's not about our best interests. We have to love ourselves enough, not to become a victim to the many negative situations that we find ourselves in, from time to time. The only time I had regrets was when I stopped believing in myself, and the decisions that I'd made. These were soon elevated, once I'd understood and reconnected to my truth, and trusted in myself, once more.

The thoughts of self-doubt only became evident when I strayed from the source of my higher self and that of my truth. At these times I would look for the mirror images within my life to show me what was wrong. My negative thoughts kept me from moving forwards, allowing myself to fall into the trap of self-deceit. So when we can see the illusions for what they are, we'll realise that through some fear or other, we had blocked our own pathway of continued growth. So by changing the way I thought or perceived the different situation, opened new doorways, bring the many opportunities that enabled me to explore new territory.

The illusions are our negative mindsets, only seeing what we want to see, in order to fill the voids and imbalances within, allowing us to cope with certain aspects within our lives. This keeps us in our comfort zones that we've created for ourselves from the insecurities that we feel, through the lack of trust, belief and faith in our own abilities and us. The illusions of life are there in order to help us cope with the most horrendous situations, the learning's lifting the veil of deceit, once we are stronger to deal with the situations or circumstances that we've found ourselves in. The illusions were what we needed to see, enabling us to feed our negativity in allowing us to feel good about what was or wasn't happening within our everyday lives.

Our thoughts influencing our actions, not realising that we are our own worst enemy when it comes to achieving our dreams. If we wanted to fulfil our dreams for the wrong reasons, our negative thoughts would keep us locked into the belief that we were not deserving or not good enough, in some-way. The mental anguish of the soul comes from the ignorance to the power of the mind, over the body and our actions, affecting all that we do, by not understanding that what had happened to us. We allow these things to happen so that we can learn from them, all being part of our life's path and purpose.

When in mediation, our thoughts are a constant battle; we try to empty our minds so that we can be inspired by our higher consciousness. But our negative thoughts get in the way because we may-be feeling guilty that we are meditating, when we have so much that needs to be done within our everyday lives. It is very difficult to empty our minds of our thoughts, and the reason being that we lead busy lives, and we've forgotten how to relax. So our positive thoughts are suppressed, all because we've forgotten how to communicate with our higher inner-self. The negative thoughts are our lower physical self, trying to influence what we do or think, with the negative undertones of our past mistakes, and our negative traits. To be able to know the difference, we must be still and go within, if we act upon a knowing thought, it's our intuition an instinctive response that will let us know if something is right or wrong. We must trust our higher self to guide us into making the right decisions. Bearing in mind that what is right today may change tomorrow, changing with our level of conscious ability.

Mediation is a good way of disciplining our minds and thought patterns .Practicing meditative control of our thoughts, allows us the opportunity to know the difference between our lower thoughts and the higher instinctive thoughts of the higher consciousness. Again, it's about the needs and wants, when thinking about our needs, our higher thoughts bring the solutions to fulfilling them if they are about our truth. When thinking about our wants, our negative thoughts confuses the issues creating the illusions. This leaves us wanting and craving for them, for the wrong reasons, which creates the imbalance or disharmony within? Focusing on what we haven't got or may never have, creates negative tension, but to focus instead, on what we do have and already have achieved, keeps us in a more positive mindset.

Through mediation and with the power of our thoughts, we can achieve great things. We can heal our minds, body and soul; restoring faith and belief in ourselves once more, and in all that we do. We'll be able to activate our unique gifts, and talents, allowing us to perfect our abilities into achieving all that we desire. This allows us to learn the art of projection of the minds energy, which aids with the reconnection of all that we need, manifesting all that we desire. Our thoughts are very powerful, so be careful for what you wish or ask for. Even our little thoughts can be powerful; maybe thoughts that we really did not pay much attention too, but we found ourselves wishing them anyway.

Someone I knew, expressed that they needed two months off from their everyday life, to catch up with the chores that they'd been putting off. Unfortunately they had a car accident that yes, gave them two months off but not to catch up with their chores but to recuperate from their injuries. The positive side to this situation was they were given the time and space, to reflect on the different aspects of their life that they were not happy with. Then being given a chance to change things within their lives, in order to create more time for them. Just remember that our thoughts play an important part, in what happens to us, along-side our emotional insecurities and imbalances, the lessons that we needed to learn from, in order to evolve successfully.

Everything that happens to us happens for a reason. This is one of the hardest lessons to learn, because of the awful situations that do happen, at times. To understand the learning's takes commitment and courage in facing our demons or fears head on. So I will explain some of my negative experiences that have caused me anguish and concern. Through the art of kinesiology I found out that at conception my thoughts were that I did not want to be born into this lifetime to face the anguish of my lessons all over again. In order to face my fears I was shown the overall desired outcome of what I was to accomplish, these were part of my desires and dreams. I was also shown aspects of my true destiny but first, I had to overcome my life's purpose which would set me free to achieve the ultimate dream.

I was born into this lifetime with the knowing of all events, situations and the solutions to my problems, all stored within my sub-conscious. The solutions would be revealed to me, when the time became right for me to know more about how I was in control of my life and destiny. But first, I had to recognise and overcome the obstacles of my lessons, and when they were fully understood and overcome, I was then able to unleash my full potential, allowing me to enjoy the secrets and new found state of awareness that enabled me to be successful in all I did.

So as a small child and feeling disconnected from life, only now realising that it was not from life that I was disconnected from, but my truth and inner-self. Because of this disconnection throughout my early years I felt vulnerable, becoming fearful of the dark shadows all of which were created from the illusions of my negative mindset. We all have two sides to our character, the negative and the positive. So my positive side naturally came into play, allowing me to be who I truly was, but not all of the time. This is why we search all of our lives for our inner truth, the positive aspects of the real us. Because with the reconnection to our true selves, helps us achieve happiness, contentment and fulfilment, on every conscious level of our Being. While I was growing up, I was aware of feeling different but didn't understand what it was all about. We go through the process of living our lives, being influenced by our thoughts, programming, beliefs and concepts. So we do what we had pre-agreed to do, the difference being is in how we perceive the situations that happens to us. Hand on heart, with every decision that I have ever made, I truly believed at that time that they were the right choices. It's only when things started to go wrong, did I consider whether I had made the right decisions or not. Procrastination of the self, through self-doubting is when the negative side of our nature takes over, and our life's lessons begin. So by not believing in us anymore, the battle of our thoughts confuses the issues. This can create the solutions to our problems that elude us, until we realise that we can reconnect to the ultimate power within, which then allows us to be in control of our thoughts and true-destiny. We can then let go of the negative doubts about us, and take positive action into achieving our goals.

After my first divorce and when things had not turned out the way I had been led to believe or hoped for. I lost faith in human nature, not being able to trust others or life and I became very fearful of making any decisions, also I had a fear of failure, rejection and betrayal. So my negative mindset kept me down, my positive thoughts was dismissed, because of my fear base. I then created a comfort zone, telling myself anything in order to feel safe and secure. The negative mindsets made me feel not good enough, not deserving, and that the good things in life did not happen to me. I began to dislike myself, thinking that I was unlovable. So as you can see, my negative thoughts did their work, keeping me in a place of defeat until the time became right for me to come back up fighting. This is when I started my inner journey into rediscovering my true self, the person that I'd always known myself to be.

My thoughts then became positive thoughts, and taking one step at time because to look at the task as a whole was quite frightening. To break it down into small pieces and achievable steps, enabled me to cope with the lessons and there understandings, and move forwards with my life confidently. My thoughts would then inspire me, allowing myself to act upon the information given. At first, it was with half-hearted attempts because of the lack of courage, but with a more positive approach I started to make progress. When we realise that what we give out, is what we get back, good or bad. This allows us to become more thoughtful of our actions, by understanding the different situation allows us to be more accepting of what's happening within our lives.

With a positive mindset we can achieve anything we want, but also to recognise what we've already achieved or accomplished, being proud of ourselves because by not recognising our achievement leaves us feeling unfulfilled. All thoughts must become positive thoughts, allowing us the opportunity of getting our lives back on track. When all is said and done, what we make of our lives is up to us, we do have choices to whether we allow ourselves to stay in the negative situations or to turn our lives around, by our positive thoughts and actions.

I do not regret any of the situations or circumstances that I had found myself in, only now being able to rejoice the positive aspects from those times and there learning's. My thoughts had played a big part in allowing me to understand my demises, helping me to recognise that all that happened was all part of the divine plan, and the reconnection of my truth. This made me realise how lucky I'd been and privileged to gain greater understanding, and in-sight into my life's purpose. This has allowed me to go on my life's journey, fulfilling my dreams and goals.

When we become fully accepting of whom we truly are, our thoughts are positive signals, messages, and instructions from the higher self, which requires observation and action. Being able to successfully understand what our higher consciousness is telling us would enable us to pursue our dreams and desires, in earnest and naturally. Not feeling threatened in anyway, if at first our dreams are not realised or achieved. Allowing us to be more accepting that the time may not be right or there is something that we had not yet fully understood. Or simply that we needed to elevate an imbalance or blockage first which allows us to be more accepting. Only then are we able to achieve what we desired but in a positive mindset, and for the right reasons. This process is guaranteed to give us back, full control of our everyday life.

Destiny and self-effort will propel us forwards into achieving our dreams, allowing the positive attributes of the real us, to shine and radiate into every aspect of our lives. We are never alone, because our thoughts will keep us company, and we may not always like what we're being told, but with faith, trust, and belief in our true self, we can accomplish our goals successfully.

When we give into our negative thoughts, we become down and depressed, and the only person to change our demise is our-self, so before the negative imbalance creates problems for us, do something about it. Any positive thought or action will give you an opportunity to understanding your life's lessons and then enables you to move onto, better times.

Have you ever stopped to think how many thoughts we have in a day? It must be a thousand plus. The more positive thoughts that we have, will be multiplied by our good fortune, and when we have positive thoughts about ourselves on a daily basis, will enhance our well being. We will then develop new thought patterns, and with daily affirmations can transform our lives, by giving us back the control in maintaining a healthy mind, body and soul. This allows us to heal all past trauma and negativity, restoring balance and harmony within all aspects of our lives, and when we accept all that's within our life, enables health to become a natural state, by nourishing the mind, body and soul. We will then be open to receiving all that we need instinctively giving us abundance with our lives once more.

Our positive thoughts is the deed, so when we send positive thoughts to our loved ones that are ill or in trouble, know that they'll receive help because you've tapped into the collective conscious vibration. The power of prayer creates positive vibrations for all of those in need, allowing them to receive the help that's required. We are not God, so we cannot change what happens to others, but the power of our prayers or thoughts helps them to be more excepting of their demise or to receive healing. This also allows them, the opportunity to tap into the infinite energy of our universe, granting them the ultimate knowledge and wisdom, to endure and understand their problems or lessons, not just of this lifetime but other lifetimes too.

Nothing is by chance, everything happens in the divine order; we all have the knowledge and wisdom within, helping us to achieve great things. Our thoughts are influencing us every step of the way. God does not desert us in our hour of need; we do, through lack of faith, trust and belief in ourselves. At the moment of death what would our last thought be? I believe its joy and happiness to be going home, but most of all; we would become all knowing once more, and our truth will be recognised, making us feel whole and complete.

The higher consciousness of our thoughts lives on within the Akasha records and Esoteric knowledge of the higher consciousness recorded for prosperity. We will all be able to recall this information when it is required, whether in an incarnate form or the soul of our true essence. As a human form we have thoughts, but as a soul we become all knowing. Life's purpose is not to think in a human form, but to reconnect with the soul and to become All Knowing. We then live the life that we've all aspired too, with the reconnection to the soul brings prosperity into this lifetime. This allows us to embrace all that we do have within our lives, at a time where we're struggling with the insecurities of our present climate.

Prosperity allows us to thrive within every area of our lives; to be prosperous brings many riches, but first we need to free ourselves from all restraints and restrictions that we hold us too, and then allow ourselves to soar to great heights. The higher our vibrations take us, the greater our understanding will be, and the deliverance into this wondrous world of power and intention. The truth of our thoughts is to be living a heavenly life but in a human form.

CHAPTER 9

ILLUSIONS OF LIFE

What are our illusions in life all about? In past lifetimes we had issues and conflicts that affected our mind, body and soul. On our deaths the negative vibrations of which was carried forwards, because within any lifetime the demise of our death, will be a direct result of an emotional imbalance or suppressed anxiety that we had stored within. We then allow these imbalances to manifest into an illness or disease taking its toll on the physical body. Which adds to the mental pressure, and exhaustion of us trying to adjust to the circumstances that we've found ourselves in?

With all illusions of life they are about our miss-perception, of how we view the different situations and circumstances within our lives that cause us concern. So our life's purpose is to overcome these imbalances of all lifetimes, so that we can understand and eradicate the disharmonious imbalances from within. Which will enable us to live a long and healthy life, dying naturally when our time on earth, is over? We must try to understand the events that's happened to us, and why? Whether in this lifetime or other lifetimes, the important fact is to make amends within this life, to allow us to achieve our full potential. If we're ill or trying to overcome a disease, brings disruption within our lives at a time when we are already struggling, with just surviving our present climate. With the accumulation of our negative traits of all that we've ever done, and to what is now stopping us from accomplishing Well Being.

The emotional issues within our lives, creates physical and mental problems, which causes us to be in a mental fog that will not allow us, to see what is really real. Out of emotional anguish we allow ourselves to be temporarily blinded by what we need to be real, in order to function within our daily lives. Justifying our needs and wants, totally oblivious to the truth of what is really going on. How many times have we said we are ok, when we are not? Not being able to recognise the imbalances or disharmony within until it becomes too late. Our higher consciousness lets us know when we're not acting, speaking or even hearing our truth. When our emotions run wild out of desperation, we make others or even the different situations a projection of our insecurities, focusing on them, because it distracts us from ourselves. Not realising the illusions of only seeing what we want to see, and dismissing the unrest of our inner-self and that of our soul.

When we understand the illusions that we have created for ourselves, we can then set about alleviating the negative imbalances from within. But first, we must understand the lessons behind the delusions and to how they have affected us. We all go through life trying to understand the different lessons, only to find that we keep making the same mistakes over and over again. Attracting to us, the mirror images of ourselves, like attracts like. With all people that we meet, within them, will be an opposite negative trait of ourselves, helping us all to overcome life's lessons.

We often hear ourselves offering advice, not really listening to the hidden message for ourselves, maybe telling someone to pull their socks up or even to sort themselves out. When the fact of the matter is, we need to do the same. When we tell someone to sort their problems out, in hindsight we have problems that also need attention and needs to be sorted out sooner rather than later. If we focus on what others are doing, we are not focusing on ourselves, maybe putting off until tomorrow, what we should have achieved today. It's human nature to focus on someone else, finding fault with what they are doing or not doing. It helps us to justify our own unhappiness or the different imbalance that we feel within, and we hadn't recognised.

With our emotional insecurities creating the illusions of feelings of neglect, rejection or even feeling deserted and alone, in our times of need or wants. We give our power away by not focusing on ourselves, putting too much time and effort into the things that we have no control over. So let me explain some of my delusional experiences; when I was going through my difficult times, getting more and more frustrated with myself, often displaying inner anger, self-sabotaging my efforts. I would push myself to the absolute limits, trying harder and harder to work through my problems. Only to find I was still blocked on a sub-conscious level, so I would stop focusing on me, and started the process of pushing others to be succeed. This mindset went on for quite a few years, only I did not know that's what I was doing at that particular time.

So when my life had not moved on the way I had hoped for, I began to look for the reasons as to why, often blaming others or the different situations from sear frustration. Others had not asked me to make them my main priority focus, unknowingly I'd just had. This was because it made me feel better about me or the illusion that I was doing something with my life, which then created a temporary distraction, all because I'd not recognised what my insecurities were all about. I often felt guilty at doing nothing for me when others were so busy within their lives. So I would find things to do realising that at times I was being a busy fool, kidding myself that just because I was working hard, I would get the rewards. This is not always so, because of the reasons behind our actions, if we're not doing things for the right reasons in what we're trying to achieve, we would then create us with a false sense of security.

The illusion behind my actions was because on a deeper level I'd not thought myself worthy of putting myself first or even loving myself enough to want better things within my life.

To crave for things is to fill the voids within, to need things is to create the illusions but to want things is because we know we are worthy of them. When I let go of my fears this allowed me to move forwards, allowing me to pursue the interests that best suited my skills and talents. When in a state of unhappiness we block our creative side, so we can never really appreciate our natural gifts, skills and abilities. To enjoy your work or vocation, would give you fulfilment, making you realise how lucky you were to be doing a job that brings you great satisfaction.

So the illusions in life allow us to delude ourselves, into thinking everything is okay, even though we can feel the disharmony within. I remember thinking once; just after my first marriage failed that I could not allow myself to cry because I was afraid that I would never stop. So I put the lid on my emotions, thinking that I was in control, how wrong I was it created even more unrest for my soul. Later, finding out that others had perceived my situation thinking that I'd coped with the breakup of my marriage, and I was strong, so they thought that I was okay and didn't need help. The illusions were there for all to see; only I was not alright, so until I asked for help, my unhappy state continued. The unhappiness that I'd created was so intense that I wanted out of this lifetime but that was not to be, because I'd agreed to sort it all out this time. My life's purpose helped me to achieve my lessons, by facing my demons head on; otherwise I couldn't reach my full potential.

Other illusions were about self-preservation, only seeing what I wanted to see, in order to function on a day to day basis. Keeping me in a comfort zone where I needed to protect myself from the truth, in fear that I wouldn't cope. The truth was, I was not coping anyway, and I was just kidding myself into thinking everything was ok. On a sub-conscious level I was actually punishing myself, keeping myself locked into situations that really were not beneficial to my Well Being. I kept myself busy because to face my truth at that particular time was just too painful, because I was fearful of getting it wrong, all over again. Strange though it may seem, procrastination is a powerful tool to self-destruction. I actually did push my self-destruct button, closing down on myself, thinking that what was happening to me, I was being punished in some-way. I just went along with it, thinking that I had no choice and that I was not destined to be truly happy. Things within my life were not as I wanted or perceived for myself. So when the time became right, and I was stronger to deal with the negative emotions, I began the slow process of sorting it all out. It's at this point that you realise the extent of the illusions, in removing the veil of deceit from my eyes, enabled me to see the truth about the different situations and circumstances that had been within my life, and were all part of my life's purpose.

At first it was a daunting task, mainly because I felt stupid having allowed myself to be deceived in the first place. When I found out that my main life's lesson had been about denying myself on every level of my Being, I must admit I was relieved. Giving in, to the excitement of realising that the choices I had made, were in-fact the right choices, experiencing the unhappy times in order to learn from them. It is only after the realisation, and with the reconnection to our truth about the reasons behind our thoughts or actions that we truly appreciate our authentic self. Lifting the veil of deceit, seeing the illusions for what they really were. With the realisation of how my lower consciousness and that of the pride and ego, had kept me in a negative mindset. Illusions are false beliefs, making ourselves believe in the poor-me syndrome.

We delude ourselves into feeling better, mistakenly believing we are unhappy when in-fact we're not. We are only unhappy because we'd not understood what our unhappiness was all about. The negative imbalances and disharmony within that was created from the emotional upsets that we'd not fully understood or dealt with correctly. This allows the lower consciousness to store the negative undertones within, creating the aliments, illness or even some disease, taking its toll on our physical body. All brought on, through the cause and effect of our actions or thoughts. The mind is a powerful tool, influencing the body which then responds in a negative or positive way, to the many disharmonious situations that we find ourselves in. With the veil of deceit clouding our judgements, actions and interactions with all things, makes our lives very difficult, leaving us struggling with even just the simplest of things in life.

So the next time you find yourself in a disharmonious situation, try understanding the illusions. Are you focusing on someone else, because you'd not recognised your own imbalances within? What we say to others we can usually take on-board for ourselves, learning the lessons also. So if we accuse someone of not loving us enough that's because we do not love ourselves enough. If we are resentful in what we are doing, it's because we are doing them, for the wrong reasons. If we are fed up with life, we are fed up with ourselves and need to reinstate harmony.

The mirror images that come from the illusions are there to help us all see, reality. The constant battles into these intensified issues leaves us struggling with the most menial tasks. This causes us to show signs of fatigue, low self-esteem, no self-worth or even a lack of confidence in ourselves and the decisions that we make. To justify our actions is basically saying we are wrong in some-way, we end up by giving our power away, allowing us to be deceived. The illusions are part and parcel of our pride and ego. Right from an early age we would have allowed the lower conscious self to rule supreme, all because we did not know of the higher self, and the power of the higher consciousness. So next time we find ourselves having the conflicting issues of what is right or wrong, allow the veil of deceit to be lifted, so that we can see what's real.

The higher consciousness is the unique power of divinity; its connection to our higher-self and true-self, which gives us back control of our true-destiny. Accessing the carbon footprint of our lifetime and all other lifetimes makes us a powerful Being. The higher consciousness allows us access to the greater knowledge and wisdom, enabling us to see through the different illusions of life. With the realisation of this in-sight, will then enable our vibration to rise, giving us healing on a higher conscious level. This healing of the mind, body and soul, brings the realignment of all our positive attributes of whom we have ever been, along with the universal and earths energy. This allows us to recognise and become our unrealised potential, making us a limitless Being, by becoming whole and complete once more.

Our life's purpose is to overcome the illusions of how we had wrongly perceived our lives to be, whether in this lifetime or previous lifetimes, God did not intend for us to be unhappy. It's only our insecurities that allow the unhappiness to manifest, within the different aspects of our everyday lives. We are all here, in order to overcome our miss-judgements of how we perceive our unhappiness, and to how we had allowed it to affect us. We will then understand that we are not hard done, allowing us to rejoice in all that we have achieved and accomplished within our lives. We can change the way we think, feel and react to the negativity within our learning's.

God gave us the freedom of choice, and the chance to change all that we do not like or want, within our lives. But not at the detriment to others, in other words, it's not acceptable to off-load our problems, insecurities or to blame others, for our demises. We have to take full responsibility for our actions and outcomes, knowing and feeling comfortable with who we truly are. To fully understand the different aspects within our life's lessons, the philosophy of which can take us to the higher conscious levels of awareness. To push the boundaries of our conscious abilities, allows us to attain the new levels of understanding of our life purpose, gaining even deeper levels of consciousness. Naturally allowing ourselves the opportunity to raise our conscious ability and awareness, where everything within our lives will be dealt with on a much higher level of consciousness. A vibration where miracles and incredible experiences of the paranormal happen, becoming a part of our everyday life and us.

The number one illusion is in thinking we are hard done too. The second is to think we have no choice. The third is to allow ourselves to stay ignorant to the possibility that what is in-fact happening to us, was meant to happen. We have all agreed to the different situations being played out within our lifetimes, in order for us to gain a deeper understanding of our life's purpose of all lifetimes. With the acceptance of this information, would allow us to set ourselves free from the imbalances and disharmony within. The veils of the illusions are there for us all to see, but only when we are prepared to take back that control of our pre-agreed destiny.

With this evolutionary cycle of great possibilities, the opportunities and challenges are given to us every day in every-way, for us to experience life to the full. We must all play our parts of removing the veil of deceit from our eyes, and to see the things we had not recognised as being our greatest gifts of the self. To manifest a life that surpasses all other expectations is a life full of promise and surprises. The illusions playing an important part of what we think is real, allowing us to realise what is really real. When we have exposed the truth of all situations within our lives, our thoughts, actions and deeds become pure. Enabling us to enjoy all aspects of our lives, showing gratitude for the wonderful gifts that we've already have within our lives, and to what we still have to accomplish. But more importantly, rejoicing in the opportunities given, in allowing ourselves to see life with love, light and truth.

CHAPTER 10

INCARNATION & CALIBRATION OF THE SOUL

Incarnation helps in the continuance of the soul's development, as we choose the lifetime that we need to be born in, and where the situations or circumstances perfectly match our lessons that we need to learn and overcome. As we evolve, we develop our instinctive behavioural patterns, important to our survival. During the soul journey through the different lifetimes, we have found ourselves dismissing these unique gifts, as no longer being relevant to our continued spiritual or personal growth. Through the process of living our lives over the many centuries, we've lost touch with some of our intuitive and instinctive innate impulses. Our natural responses to the different situations that would have lead us away from danger or pain being inflicted, which would have helped us to achieve our soul's purpose a lot quicker.

When we become disconnected from these natural gifts, will result in our lack of trust within our true-selves this will stop us from achieving our full potential? The disconnection of our truth as prevented us from being in touch with the information that would have helped us to understand the circumstances, behind the different events has they happen to us? This would have helped us realised the vital information that would allow us to be accepting, and also gives us the understanding of why we must learn from our life's lessons. With the help of our unique gifts our instinctive reactions will reveal the information that's important to our soul's growth. Helping us with the continuance of the soul's journey evolving through time, whilst exploring and expanding our boundaries of awareness, to the greater understanding of what our lives are all about. The souls purpose is to achieve our full potential; unleashing our unique selves that enables the reconnection of the higher conscious self, and that of our soul. In achieving the soul's calibration of continued growth, we will attain the ultimate state of existence, whilst here on the earth plane. This would then grant us with the experience a heavenly life, in a human form.

Through the centuries we have experienced the evolutionary changes in our present climate, population, form, economic growth and so on. Completing cycles and repeating history, but what did we learn? We learned what the textbooks taught us, the interpretations of some great philosophers or scholars of our times. They gave an insight into the vision of inspired people, who had greater awareness about the philosophy to living a life, successfully. The interpretation of the soul is about each individual's personal journey of their soul's quest, the visionary in-sight into their history records.

Our soul is the time traveller who's connected to the collective memory of all that is, and it teaches us, all that we need to know? Each and every-one of us is a part of the conscious energy of all that we've ever been, to help us know what we've experienced and must overcome. We can only activate information that is relevant to each lifetime when it's needed, because the collective memory is so powerful that it would blow us away. Some of the most enlightened souls have to retreat from society, because they vibrate at such a high vibrational level, they could not cope with the simple mundane tasks of life. Their vibration being so refined that sudden shocks or exposure to an ordinary life could cause then harm or extinction. This is why the Guru's of our times are heavily guarded and protected, to maintain an earthly existence.

Could it really be that simple, connection to the higher consciousness and we are enlightened, no, like everything in life, we have to work hard to achieve it. That's why it takes many lifetimes to complete, as we started the soul's journey a very long time ago. We need to realise that we've now entered a time of the Spiritual Evolutionary Age, and for whatever reason, whether it's cyclic, we are all being made aware of our imbalances and disharmony within. We are being made aware of, and given access to our natural gifts and abilities that will allow us, to deal with these changes that we are being made to make. Spirituality is readily accepted with alternative cultures and remedies being pursued in alleviating our problems. With self-help books covering a wide range of subjects, and are now being read by the majority. The works of some very enlightened people guiding us along the way. Just allow yourself to be drawn to what you need, nothing happens by chance, and all that you need is provided for.

Our soul's purpose is about setting ourselves free from the restraints, restrictions, beliefs and concepts that we hold ourselves too. In achieving this, we would allow our higher consciousness, the Soul of our higher self, to rule supreme. To have total faith in our mystical gifts, skills and abilities, helps us to achieve the ultimate state of consciousness. This then enables us to achieve our full potential, what does that mean? For some it means that they will fulfil their dreams, others travelling an enlightened pathway, will achieve things beyond their wildest dreams. They will attain the enlightened status of the Soul, going on to pursue great achievements, experiencing incredible powers, strength and abilities. Becoming All Knowing, and having inner vision that foretells or prophesies future events, disasters or even to inspire us, with the greater Knowledge and infinite Wisdom of all lives.

We are just a small fragmentation of our true selves, not becoming whole until we have reconnected with the truth of our soul. Our truth being the infinite knowledge and wisdom held within our sub-conscious. My soul shows it's self through my spiritual guides, each guide, being a true representation of my truth. During my inner journey, I have encountered different guides within the different levels of awareness. They all guide, and encouraged me through the different stages of my spiritual growth, and the lessons that I needed to learn.

119

With each aspect or lesson that I have learnt, so I was introduced to the next guide and so on. My spiritual growth has taken me many years to get even this close, to the understandings of all that I have attained so far. I know that it's going to take me, many more years to come or even lifetimes, before I complete the journey of my soul's quest. Even then, searching for the continued quest or even for the soul to be able to take the well-earned rest, attained at the higher levels of consciousness, within the kingdom of heaven.

I have worked with forty-two of my spiritual guides to date; each and every-one of us an army of spiritual guides, helping us achieve our true potential. The guide that I am working with at the moment is a philosopher, helping me to translate what I've learned to the best of my ability, and comprehend the information given. It never ceases to amaze me, how the learning's expands my mind's energy, the more of the minds energy that we use, the more we have at our disposal. Our peripheral abilities give us greater in-sight into our soul's calibrated journey.

Everything within our lives happens for a reason, it's all part of the divine plan and our life's purpose. Every last detail is pre-thought, agreed and planned. When the time becomes right, we do what we need to do, in order to evolve successfully. So if you have found yourself reading any self-help book, there will be a reason as to why. If you can only relate to just a small part of the information given, then you have exposed yourself to the higher vibrations, which allows you to continue on your own spiritual journey through life. By being open to receiving, you will then be in a position to give to others, sharing the knowledge that then accesses the wisdom. Our souls are the higher consciousness of our thoughts, actions, feelings and our instinctive behavioural patterns. They are also the characteristics and inherited traits that make us all individual, giving us our unique personalities.

The mirror images in life tell us so much about what's going on, and to what's required from us. The synchronicities of life, allows the universe to give you all that you need, and allows us a life that just flows. The coincidences of life, gives us the opportunity to get the most out of our lives, when faced with the many opportunities or challenges. We should rejoice and be grateful for everyone and everything that we hold dear. Enjoy your time, exploring and enjoying the adventures that we seek in order to experience our lives to the full. We really do have a lot to be thankful for, saviour the memories of bygone time, just imagining yourself in another lifetime and to what you may have been doing? We must appreciate all walks of life, because you would have experienced it all at sometime or other.

To show compassion, enables us to understand the events that we may not have experienced in this lifetime, but have experienced them in another incarnation, long ago. I had a lifetime back in the early nineteen hundreds which resulted in my death, I was murdered. This life was hard because of the poverty that I found myself in, having children and working as a chorus girl, my mindset was of being hard done too. This was because of not much money, and only having the bare basics to live off. I was murdered because I became a victim to my situation, all of which was pre-agreed; I was reborn in 1953 why? Because, in the previous life I felt hard done too, that life was hard work, and the struggle became too much. In this lifetime I had an easy first 46 years (This was the age when I died in the previous life), my life this time around was very rewarding but then through the choices that I'd made, I became a victim of my own doing. I began to struggle with every aspect of my life; the lack money was a big issue. From having a privileged life-style to having to adjust to the bear-minimum was really difficult; coming down the social ladder was a soul breaking time. I felt at times that I would not recover from the breakdown of my marriage, no home or job; it really was a lot to bear, even if it was my choice, but the choices of others also took its toll on me.

My spiritual journey allowed me to reconnect with my truth, which enabled me to accept my situation and circumstances. The overall lesson was ACCEPTANCE, if I had trusted and believed in my true-self, I would have realised that everything within my life was how it should be. To allow myself to overcome my life's purpose was to live the life that I'd pre-agreed too that would enable me to reconnect to my truth. So therefore, I followed the pathway that allowed me to experience all that I needed too, in order to gain the deeper fundamental learning's of my soul. This puts us in a privileged position of trust, faith and total acceptance of the real us. Knowing that sometime in the future, and another part of my life's story will unfold, and it will allow me, the opportunity to gain even greater knowledge of my intended life.

There have been case studies of people who can recall past lifetimes, reliving the events, situation or circumstances that they'd once found themselves once in. Children are renowned for talking about when they had other lives; other mommy's or daddy's being able to give quite accurate details. But what is it all about? It's to enable us to understand our life's purpose. There is no particular time scale to when we will be reborn, just the determination of the soul. I had a reincarnation where I came straight back; my life had been cut short, so I came straight back, being able to carry on with the learning's within that particular century. So the memories that we sometimes recall are from the sub-conscious, memories that we had requested to be played out within this lifetime, when we need them to remind us of the details of our pre-agreement. Helping us to achieve a deeper understanding of our life's purpose and to what our lives are all about. The information received is with the sole intention of us reliving an aspect of a previous lifetime, in order to overcome a life's valuable lesson, within this one. This will grant us with the

greater knowledge, enabling the infinite \
forwards on our continued journey to enligh.

The higher consciousness is the n
important information, so to reconnect wi.
consciousness gives us the ultimate power c
talked about the illusions that we hold ourselves .
just a diversion from the truth. We have allowed c
be misled by our lower conscious self, but they also .
deep rooted emotions that need to be dealt with. It c
be unnerving to think there could be other lifetimes, le
dimensions. But you can be assured, we are not
anything that we cannot cope with, this is just another le\
awareness.

The journey of the soul is not in how many lifetimes w
have had, but about how many successful lifetimes that we've
had. As I have said before, God did not intend for us to lead
unhappy lives, he only wants us to achieve peace and
harmony, with us living in unity. So the purpose of the soul's
quest is to achieve that unity. We do not have to make the
soul's quest difficult for ourselves, with our endless struggles,
all because we've paid very little attention to the souls needs.
We spend a lot of time and money on the body, with the poor
mind or soul being over looked, perhaps thinking that we didn't
have too until we feel the unrest within. We are all being made
aware that's it is now time for us all, to become realigned with
the mind, body and soul; so we can all move onto better times.

We all have free will and freedom to choose what we
want out of life, but we must listen to our inner self, as this
enable us to become open-minded and allow our gut reactions
to lead us forwards. But not with fear or trepidation within our
hearts, as this stops us from trusting our true self, to guide us
forwards. We have choices that we need to make that are in
accordance of the evolutionary journey, to enable the
reconnection with your true essence of our soul, granting us
with the control of our true destiny. For our soul knows the

and is all knowing, so allow your soul to guide you ards, and within the essence of our soul holds the carbon print of all existences.

Our higher consciousness speaks to us through our oughts, then influencing our physical body and decisions. he purpose of the soul is to guide us successfully into the wenty-first century. This will enable us to live the life that was ntended for us, enjoying our world while we still have time, pursuing our dreams, bringing them into reality. So allow yourself to reconnect with your higher consciousness and to become still and know. For deep within our soul is the answers that we seek. The lesson of the Soul is to enjoy living our lives to the full, in Love, Light and Peace.

Our soul's calibration is the acumination of the different aspect of our true-selves and of who we have ever been. The characteristics of each incarnate form, is what makes us all individual and unique. We will carry the genetic similarities of our personalities and inherited traits, through each incarnate lifetime. All relevant details, is recorded within the palms of our hands, the unique information of who and what we have ever done, and to what we can actually achieve. They carry the details of past, present, and future events, telling us of the negative traits that we must understand and elevate. In-fact they hold the important information that once recognised will set us free, allowing us to act upon our intuitive natures to guide us forwards through our lifetime. This will enable us to achieve our full potential, and to become a limitless being. We have everything we need to live the life that was intended, our mental, physical and spiritual being, realigned to the earth's and universal energy, and this sustains all growth.

CHAPTER 11

THE SPIRIT WORLD

The spirit world is where we return too, after every incarnation of the soul. We return to the source of infinite energy and that of our Creator. So after every lifetime we would return back to the source, in order to rediscover the purpose of our life, whilst here on the earth plane. We need to understand and see if we achieved our pre-agreement, and to see if we've realised or even reached our full potential. We would also find out if we had understood all aspects of the agreement that we made, before we was born into this lifetime. They were the detail of our lessons that we had promised to overcome, in order to evolve successfully. The memory of that agreement was then stored deep within our sub-conscious, waiting for the time to become right, so that the sequence of events could unfold so we could learn and evolve from.

The Spirit World is another dimension of this world; it's a world that runs parallel with our earthly world. The kingdom of eternal bliss, the manifestation of all dreams, our true home and infinite energy of the life force and Creator of all that is. The Spirit World (or heaven as it's more commonly known) is where the weary soul goes to rest, some of us, having to overcome the trauma of death or the emotional issues and anxieties of our departed life. So we can attain the understanding of the cause and effects, of our decisions or actions. Which then resulted in the unrest within, whilst living our earthly life? To enable us to fully appreciate all that we'd accomplished, and to see if we had achieved a greater understanding of our life's purpose. The lessons and their unique learning's would have allowed us to gain an in-sight into our soul's purpose and the reconnection to the higher brations. Which would have enabled us to attain an enlightened status, and the understanding of the collective consciousness of humankind?

On return to the spirit world our deceased loved ones are waiting to greet us, our soul returning home. To be taken care of, while evolving back to the vibration of our true essence and that of our truth, this allows us to become a part of the ocean of infinite energy, once more. If you relax and close your eyes, imagine what you've perceived heaven to be! It's a place where there is no suffering, no wars and no hardships. A place where you could be blissfully happy, doing all of the things that you've always dreamed of. No bad weather, only sunshine and flowers, beautiful scenery, the vibration feeling light, bright and breezy, everyone being blissfully happy.

The Spirit World and how we perceive it is just like here on the earth plane, depending on what has happened to us and to how we feel, denotes our perception of whether it's heaven or hell. Within each and every-one of us is good or bad, but also the unique ability to know right from wrong. We are all a product of the things that we've done, and then depending on how we've perceived us or the situation, will be a reflection of our truth. We are given many opportunities to make amends or to ask for forgiveness. God does not judge us, we judge ourselves, and also he doesn't punish us, we all punish ourselves un-necessarily. To forgive the self is the greatest gift we can do for us, because it sets us free from the restraints and restriction that we've placed within our lives.

The spirit world is a place of heavenly peace, harmony and grace; all who resides there live in Unity. I believe there are no new souls has we're all recycled, and we've been on the earth plane since time began. We live in a dimensional universe, one life at a time with the influence of many, affecting and inspiring all that we do. When we understand our soul's purpose, we'll realise that we've lived before and the soul's quest is to integrate with all aspects of us.

126

We can communicate with the spirit world through a medium and they relay messages from our loved ones who have passed to the other side. Their communication confirms that the soul does live on, and there is life after death. During my many years of pursuing a spiritual pathway, I have encountered many departed souls eager to keep in touch with us by passing on messages of continued love and support.

I have also received messages from my spiritual guides, guardian angels, my deceased loved ones, as well as others. Their main purpose has always been about our welfare, encouraging and comforting us, when we were in need, and they would never interfere with our lives, only wishing to inspire and support us with the choices or decisions that we make. The spirit of our loved ones draw close with the sole intention of giving us the continued advice, support and encouragement that they'd always given to us, even when on the earth plane.

It's important that we all gain the vibrational understanding of our learning's that has a positive effect on everyone concerned, because as on earth we are required to learn even when in heaven. The continued learning's are part of our soul quest in order for us all to gain an even deeper understanding of life's purpose, and to successfully continue our soul's journey. After our deaths we then wait until another lifetime as been pre-agreed, and we set off on our soul's quest all over again, to see if we can successfully live the life, that God intended for us in the first place. We must all overcome our problems without all the hardships and suffering that we create for us, whilst trying to understand what our existence on earth is all about.

When we return to the source, its purpose enables us, to see what we've understood, and to what level of awareness of our collective consciousness we've achieved. We came into this lifetime with our conscious level already set, with the view to raise our consciousness, once we'd understood and overcome our lessons, gaining a greater conscious awareness. In heaven we are required to become our truth and higher consciousness once more, having faced our truth regarding the lifetime we've just had.

The calibration of our soul de-notes our collective conscious ability and guarantees the continuance of our soul's journey. When in the spirit world we would be able to continue our studies, in the hall of knowledge, and the temples of wisdom, seeking advice from the elders and supreme beings. Really no difference from here on earth, everything that we need to know, can be found or acquired. So when we decide to return to earth to achieve those life lessons all over again, everything has already being pre-agreed so that we can evolve successfully. The knowledge and wisdom, our skills and abilities, are already set in place within our hearts and souls, waiting for the right time for them to be activated. So with our lifetime agreed and set in motion, our journey of the soul's quest begins all over again.

In our agreement, we will have pre-agreed to our parents, because their weakness or lessons that they have come to learn will be our strength. They will perfectly match our imbalances that we've already in place, deep within us. A long with the vibrations of the different events or situations, our mindsets and beliefs, in-fact everything within our characteristics that will allow us, to overcome our lessons. We will also have accepted the conditions and circumstances, right down to every last detail of our partners, siblings, families and also that of friends and acquaintances. We will have agreed to where we would live, to our lifestyles and vocations, to the sequence of events that would unfold, all of which would influence our choices and decisions. Also to the different opportunities and challenges that would change our lives forever, if recognised, understood and acted upon. All opportunities that are given are in accordance to our learning's. In-fact everything would be pre-destined, waiting for the right time to be played out, the sequence of events that creates the opportunities and challenges in life. With life's extraordinary coincidences and the synchronicities, we are given every opportunity to learn our life's purpose, all happening in divine timing.

So firstly, how do we and why do we, pre-agreed to these agreements? Because the agreement is our life's purpose, we need to have the different goals to aspire too, in order to live out our lives successfully. The memories or the higher consciousness, being the caretaker of all we had pre-agreed. We make these agreements because our life's purpose is to gain greater understanding into the different negative traits and the emotional insecurities that we hold ourselves too.

We must understand all that has happened within our lives so we can improve our future, enabling us to become our true selves and that of our truth, once more. So when we returned to earth for another incarnation, we go through the process of accomplishing the different aspects of our truth. When we die, we return back to the source of our creator, to be given access to the ultimate truth, in order to become All Knowing of every aspect of our lives. This happens all because we had not fully appreciated or understood our life's lessons, whilst here on the earth plane. So we're given the opportunity to understand them, once back in the spirit world. Then in a future incarnation, we will find ourselves having to experience the same or similar lessons all over again, to see if we had fully understood the lesson given, while living in a human form.

While on the earth plane, it's important to understand not just this lifetime lessons but pervious lifetimes as well. As this information is very important to our continued growth on every level of consciousness, but also it allows us to evolve to a higher vibrational level. We are here on earth as a direct result of the situations and circumstances that we did not fully understand or comprehend, but was important to our welfare, the lack of understanding actually stops us from living our lives to the full. By not fully understanding our life's lesson we are given the same situations over and over again, until we do.

Within our earthly life there are a lot of important aspects, to be taken into consideration, our problems, the ailments, illness's even that of diseases and disabilities. All of which would be a product of our emotional imbalances; we must also look at the different aspects of our understanding of our perception to what did happen to us. In-fact we would have to accept our parts played in any situation or circumstances where we may have perceived things in the wrong way. Or even to the different situations where we had created harm or inflicted pain in any way to others or even to us. So, whether here on the earth plane or back in spirit world, we would have to address every aspect of our lives, where we had not fully understood the problems that we needed to learn and overcome. We would then be able to offer forgiveness not to just us, but to all concerned for the problems we'd caused.

They say at the moment of death that our life flashes before our eyes. We are then given an opportunity to see the bigger picture of our lives, to help us fully understand our life's purpose. It's difficult whilst living our lives, and to get a true understanding of every aspect of our life's lessons. Spirituality is teaching us how to become detached from all things, whilst living an earthly life. To be detached from our life, in a way that only death can give us, because at the moment of death, we would have let go of all the anguish associated with living. This allows us to understand the deeper, meaningful aspects of our lessons and their unique learning's and benefits.

To watch someone die is quite an informative experience especially if you can stand detached, from what is in-fact, going on. Firstly the person who is dying will let go of situations, beliefs and the perceptions of the life they have been living. Secondly they will let go of all the material and financial wealth, for it no longer has a purpose, it cannot change the outcome. Thirdly they will slowly let go of the physical body and to the circumstances that they've found themselves in. Fourthly they prepare themselves for the goodbyes to their loved ones as they are getting ready to leave. One by one they will let go of their loved ones, and then the essence of that love, the unconditional love goes with them. Those left on the earth plane, mourn the loss of the person that's died. Those in the spirit world, rejoice the rebirth of the spirit that had just died, re-joining the eternal life force.

My philosophy is that the person who has died, their loss is greater, because they have lost all of us, i.e. the family, we have only lost them. With the transition to the spiritual world, the peace that prevails easies their anguish and torment, enabling them to understand the bigger picture of their lives. This gives then a feeling of peace and tranquillity, achieving an in-sight into all that is. The spiritual family of loved ones, who had passed previously, greets them into the heavenly realms, allowing them to accept and complete the transition back home.

Everything has a mirror image, whether it's in life or death; we must always look to the positives of any given situation. So for someone who had suffered, their death gives them the peace, knowing that they are no longer in pain. Someone who tragically dies is uplifted to heaven by the angels who support their transition. They are given the opportunity to come back and say their goodbyes in the sleeping state of those left behind. In our dream states we meet our departed loved one often, enjoying our memories, reliving the good times but also to be given the opportunity, to comfort one another.

Ever wonder what our ghostly encounters are all about? It is the unrest of a soul, who as unfinished business to attend too before they move onto the higher spiritual planes. They roam our earth because there is something that they need to overcome, before they can move on. There are several

131

reasons why this happens; maybe they were so close to understanding their life changing situation, before they passed. So this allows then the opportunity of not only helping themselves but also their nearest and dearest. Where they can all benefit from the learning's, but also for future generations, allowing them to gain the greater knowledge and wisdom.

Maybe the apparition of our ghostly friends is triggered by our intuitive abilities of accessing all that we need, to continue our souls journey. Some ghost, are about lost souls who had not realised they had died, roaming the earth plane until they gained deeper understanding. Or maybe it was just to stay behind, to make sure their loved ones overcame the trauma of their death before they moved on. But whatever the case, we all have choices and even in death, we can choose.

For me, even though it was a tragic situation, I watch my father die with my mother standing next to me. It was a great in-sight, into a very sensitive situation that will happen to us all, one day. But as we were standing by his bedside, we became aware of the monitors bleeping, his lifeline went flat. We knew there was no hope and that Dad had just died. But then, I became aware of his spirit leaving his body, leaving by the heart Chakra. It was just like someone had pinched Dads chest and the spirit detached. I was aware of the spiritual family all around him, here to take Dad home.

A sense of tranquillity filled the room for just a few seconds before the shock, grief and total despair took over. What I witnessed next, was the actions and interaction of my family; I stood just inside the room, to make way for my brothers and sisters who had not been by his bedside, at the moment of his passing. The sight that beheld me was the closeness of grief, as they continued to hug each other, to hug my Dad, then my mother. Again hugging Dad, this process went on for quite a few minutes and was very emotional.

As with any family that loses a beloved, we do not really stop to think about our actions, because the grief dulls our senses. We then react instinctively, allowing us to mourn and to offer comfort and support to one another. But the opposite of death is birth, so when a new child is born we rejoice, we are very happy, celebrating the safe arrival. In our joyfulness we do not stop to think of the opposite to birth, which is death, so in the spirit world which is as real as this one; they have lost someone close.

As with death, our birth is timely, the time is pre-agreed as with everything else. So like our time on earth, our time in the spirit world has the same objective and that is to be able to overcome and understand the valuable lessons that we didn't understand whilst on the earth plane. This process guarantees our evolutionary journey, and of the continuance of the soul.

It is important that we learn the significance to the understandings of what our lessons have been all about and to what it is that we have done to ourselves. Through the ignorance of what our emotional problems or issues can do to the mind and our physical bodies, sometimes leaving it too late, in order to make a difference to this lifetime. We then pay the price of Cause and Effect, by not being given the opportunity to overcome our problems, whilst still living an earthly life. The Knowledge and Wisdom of our inner truth, gives us the reasons as to why these things have happened in the first place, giving us an opportunity to learn and reinstate Well Being.

Only in accessing the higher consciousness, would we then be able to comprehend the bigger picture of life and death. Because all is eternal, all is infinite, all that's required from us, is to be able to reconnect with all that is, and reconnecting with the life force, of the universal energies and all of creation. Fear is the emotion that stops us attaining the understandings of all that is required of us. Fear of the unknown, fear of the uncertainty of living our life, as it was

133

intended. Our per-conceived ideas and thoughts, causes the imagination to run wild, and if we didn't give into our fears, we would become more trusting in our own abilities and unique gifts. To be accepting of all things, allows us to trust in our own knowledge that there is nothing to fear, except our own imaginations.

The spirit world is a retreat into a blissful state, to be within the collective energy once more. To know the sear joy that comes from non-attachment. We attach ourselves to so much whilst on the earth plane that it creates the delusions of what we think is important, from what is really important. In the spirit world, we would become our true essence, understanding the downfall of attachment to all things. All brought on, by our lack of trust within our true-selves and that of our truth. This results in our constant need, to attach ourselves to anything that creates a state of Well Being or offers security. All of which leads us away from our truth, the power within, of our true selves. The more we travel away from what is really important, the more we become disconnected from our source. Creating the unrest of the soul, a state of mental confusion of what we think our lives are all about, to what are lives have really been about.

When death comes, we are really quite relieved because our suffering will then be over. We then find ourselves back in the presence of the unconditional love, a love that is the only real healer of our pain and grief. To be loved or to feel love makes us feel better, in the presence of unconditional love, heals our hearts and soul, bringing omnipresence. Very few of us will experience unconditional love whilst here on the earth plane, but the memory of that love as us all travelling the universe trying to find and reconnect with it. Unconditional love is what we reconnect with when we have successfully understood our life's purpose and unconditional love as now hidden agenda.

The Golden Age of Aquarius will give us all the opportunity to be in the presence of God, our truth and the higher consciousness, no longer having to return back to the spirit world in order to reconnect with it. All we have to do is be still and go within; God is within each and every-one of us. A rebirth of the spirit of our soul, renews faith in ourselves, we then trust in our abilities, skills and gifts once more, allowing us to become all knowing of who we truly are. We are a representation of God, our life force energy and creator of all that is.

The spirit world is our true home; it is the place where our true consciousness resides, and we're just a small part of the collective consciousness of humankind. The spirit world is right here, just waiting for us to reconnect with in our human-form, it's within our hearts and souls. This will allow us to live within the kingdom of eternal peace, love and light.

When I dream of deceased loved ones I never travel upwards, because they are always right here just in another dimension. The gardens or places are bright and joyous; and they're always living their dreams or achieving their goals, and they appear healthy and happy. But if they came to me in order for me to learn from they appeared as I remembered them to be whilst here on the earth plane, and has they help me to learn, so they continued to learn also and overcome their lessons too.

Once our loved have visited us from the spirit world they are always eager to return. They often inspire me that they prefer to be where they are because after gaining an in-sight into what we've all done to ourselves; through the lack of our understandings we've made life on earth, hard work, with the suffering and strife. So if we can trust, and be in acceptance of all things, allows us to be more open to achieving all that we desire the life, and what was intended so long ago. But we can only achieve this when our purpose and lessons have been learned and overcome. With us enjoying all that we have within our lives with us, in pursuit our limitless potential. This will enable us to live in peace, harmony and total bliss.

The unconditional love is a sea, an ocean of love where we are totally supported by the infinite energy, the life force of energy of God, the almighty.

CHAPTER 12

THE ENLIGHTENED STATE OF AWARENESS

The transformation of the lower consciousness, to the higher consciousness and that of the higher self is quite extraordinary. Changing our lives in a way that you never dreamed of, not realising that you could actually change your whole persona? The transformation is noticeable to everyone; you become a limitless being, and access your true vibration of your authentic self, which allows you to continue on an ascended path.

Those who dedicate their lives to spiritual growth, expose themselves to the tremendous force of the universal energy that sustains continued growth, within every area of their lives. We all aspire to greater things, but in experiencing the enlightened state of awareness, rejuvenates the mind, body and soul. This will enhance your sense of survival, a willingness to become your true self, experiencing your own power of divinity. This creates an inner peace that aids in maintaining a youthful mind, body and soul. A knowing that enables you to practice non-attachment to the material world or our emotional insecurities, of the many needs and wants. With the exposure to this incredible vibration grants you with extraordinary gifts, skills and abilities, unleashing your creativity and artistic talents?

When we have fully understood and achieved our life's purpose, it will enable us to become our limitless potential. Allowing us to access our higher conscious vibration, which would help with the process of eliminating the emotional imbalances and disharmony from within? This brings alignment to our chakra system and the different levels of the corresponding bodies and organs, as described in my first book (The Essential Creativity of Awareness). On conquering our emotional states, we are able to set about; redefining the physical body's energies. Concentrating on the universal energy to revitalize our energy field, as well as the different chakra's throughout the physical body. We can then release the negativity or any blockages as they present themselves to us, sending them down into mother earth, allowing nature to neutralise them naturally.

This process allows us to achieve a state of Well Being throughout and within our unique energy system of the body's natural healing abilities. With a constant flow of universal energy, maintains health on all levels of our being. It is extremely important to know that our bodies are being constantly purified and cleansed, by the earth's and universal energy's. Attaining a constant flow of divine energy, granting a state of self-centeredness to our physical being, and the higher consciousness along with the universal laws. The ultimate knowledge and infinite wisdom, creates a power so strong that it connects us to the source of divinity, of all creation. This power enables us to become our higher self, maintaining balance and harmony within all aspects of life, giving us access to all that we need, when we need it, but more importantly, a power that is our true-self and that of our truth.

The transition from the lower consciousness, to the higher consciousness can at first make you feel in isolation; this is because of the transitional period of refinement to your energy field, but also to the new you. You become very sensitive and conscious of what you think, say or do. Because what we send out, is what we get back. With this new found state of awareness brings new challenges and opportunities into our lives, we begin to notice the changes within the way we'd perceive the different situations. We actually begin to show a lot more compassion and understanding, whilst being tolerant and kind, and caring for others more deeply than we did before.

We are no longer seeking fulfilment; and have now become whole, completing a cycle. This allows us to be totally accepting of our situation or circumstances that we find ourselves in. We no longer feeling threatened by the choices of others, and we're in perfect harmony with life. We become dedicated to world peace, to ease the suffering and hardships of others, and rejoice in all that we do have within our lives, enjoying everything for today.

When we enjoy nature, with the vibrancy of the colours, and textures, and to respect the elements and seasons, for all is interconnecting to the whole of creation. When we do this we become sensitive to all vibrations around and within us, which allows our energy system to help and inspire others. Everyone receives the benefits of our higher vibrational force, and we then respect and honour the universal laws knowing instinctively how to operate within its framework and structure, maintaining well being.

The physical body as less ailments, illnesses or aches and pains, because all negativity will now be dealt with, at a higher vibrational level. Illness and ailments disappearing, even to your eyesight improving, so that you longer need the bifocals, your senses are heightened of past, present and future events. The unexplained will become all knowing and the unknown becomes a part of your everyday life. You will be able to manifest your dreams and ambitions, bring them into reality. This allows us to achieve contentment on all levels of your conscious and spiritual awareness. You become open to receiving, which then allows you to give to others, unconditionally. We all have a charka system within which is constantly fed by the universal energy which feed these energy centres that maintain a healthy mind, body and soul.

Our higher consciousness is from the higher heart chakra upwards, connecting you to the universe. The lower consciousness is from the lower heart chakra downwards, connecting you to mother earth. When we maintain a balance between the universe and earth, it will sustain our growth whilst here on the earth plane. To know balance and harmony between all things brings you abundance in all that you seek. Allowing you to maintain balance throughout and within all the corresponding levels of your being, this will grant you, your limitless potential of all lifetimes.

Enlightened is who you become, when you have reconnected to your soul, the higher consciousness of the real you. To become all knowing is the ultimate state of awareness, the consciousness of life. We attain a level of conscious ability within all aspects of life, before going on to reconnect with the collective consciousness of all creation. When we become part of the collective consciousness we then achieve enlightenment, the natural power of divinity.

To become pure consciousness is to become, All Knowing. To be enlightened is what each individual seeks sometime throughout their lifetime. Enlightenment is when all things become encompassing, everything becoming into one, so just stop and think what this actually means? All things becoming into one, no beginnings and no endings, for life is eternal, especially when we have understood everything that we've ever done or achieved.

The collective consciousness of mankind enables the world's mass-negativity to become neutralised, but first, each individual as to play their part, of actively achieving the enlightened status to eradicate their own negativity first. Not just improving their lives immensely, but all lives, allowing the worlds negativity to eventually become eradicated, allowing us all to experience world peace and harmony. Allowing us to unite, interconnecting together in unity in the family of life, allowing us to become whole, once more.

The common purpose of all souls is to be united in all aspects of our lives, the coming together of weary souls, having spent lifetimes trying to reinstate balance and harmony between life and death. There is no difference between life and death, only our perception of thinking that in death our lives are no more. Death brings the rest-bite for the weary traveller, reconnecting us to the source of our life force, once more. This allows us to recharge the energies within our soul that we had allowed to become depleted. But also through our lack of understanding to the bigger picture of our lives and the truth, that once we've understood what's expected from us, would aid in us achieving all that we desired naturally. With us living a life having accomplished our life's purpose, gaining the enlightened status that would save us from unhappiness. We would then be able to successfully follow our dreams, manifesting all that we needed to life our lives, achieving our potential of all lifetimes.

The enlightened state of awareness is about the in-sight into the vision of the life that our creator intended for us all to experience. In simple terms he wants for us all to be happy, if we are not then it's about what we've exposed ourselves too. We are being given the opportunity to make amends, understanding what our actions have created, not just for ourselves but for others too. Everything that we have ever done was with the sole intention of improving the quality of our lives. When this has been accomplished, you would then be able to appreciate the intricate workings of our unique abilities, gifts and skills, and our uniqueness of the self is stored within, to enable us to achieve the balance and harmony that we seek within every aspect of our lives.

We have to give ourselves the opportunity to listen to the small voice within that would lead us through life without any of the external pain that causes us grief, so be still and know. We just need to be quieten, and emptying our minds of the clutter, which enables us to listen to the higher self, finding the answers or solutions to our problems. This gives us the ability to fulfil our dreams and desires, trusting in our intuitive response and gut reactions. This is our instinctive nature advising us with all that we need to know, and giving us the solutions of what to do. Once we have achieved this state of being, we would have all that we need to survive within the structure of our world. We then interconnect with all of creation, the power of divinity, and the ultimate power of all that is...So be still and know!

To be still and know what? Our pre-agreement of the destiny of our truth, for we all once knew the details of our intended life. So if we sit and allow our minds to become still and ask ourselves the question of what we want to know or achieve we can access the information. So by empting our minds of any pre-thoughts, we can then ask the question, wait and feel the response. You will receive your positive reply by an overwhelming feeling or recognition of the right course of action to take. Do not allow yourself to second guess, trust your instinctive reaction to guide you. This helps us to realise that everything we need is within, so allow yourself to carry out the response given, if it is wrong in anyway your instincts will let you know. You can then make changes allowing yourself to let your inner higher self, guide you.

With practice you can perfect your intuitive nature, allowing it to become a big part of your success to getting your life back on track. We have everything we need within, maintaining all that we desire. Do not be afraid to make decisions on what we know to-day and then being able to change our minds tomorrow if we have to. These are the steps that we take every-day to help us successfully live our lives to the full. If we do not make decisions we are in-fact saying we want things to stay the same. Our higher consciousness allows us the pathway to an enlightened state of awareness that then opens up other pathways for us to eventually achieve Enlightenment.

CHAPTER 13

THE FUTURE

At this present time we are all questioning what is to happen in the near and distant future. I have children and grandchildren; I find the prospects for them, very daunting. The only sure thing that we can change is our perception and attitude, of how we are going to deal with the current state of affairs. They say that everything happens for a reason, so what is it all about? It has been prophesied that our world is going to experience some dramatic changes. With the earth's magnetic field weakening, along with the prediction of the reversal of the north and south poles, is cause for concern. This results in dramatic climate changes and natural disasters such as earthquakes, volcanoes erupting and worldwide flooding, leaving us with devastation and disruption to our lives.

These disasters are already happening with flooding becoming a big problem, our climates changing dramatically, and we'll see a lot of natural catastrophic changes to our planet, with us all having to adjust. The Age of Aquarius is about the cleansing and purification of our planet, also with a spiritual transition period of the purification and cleansing of humankind. The biggest climate change at present is our rain fall and flooding, causing problems for quite a lot of people with them having to readjust their lives. In fact we are all being made aware of the natural changes that we all need to make, in order to continue our life on earth.

At present we are all struggling with the different aspect of our lives, not being sure of what to do, with the majority of us struggling on a day to day basis, with the fears of how are we going to cope, putting our heads down, is not always the best solution of thinking that this time will pass. We seem to go from crisis to crisis, but why? Are we really out of control or is time running out. To be accepting of what in-fact is going on within our lives, will make it easier for us to adjust. To alter our perception to the different situations or circumstances that we find ourselves in; will release us, from the controls that we hold ourselves too. We must have courage and take back the control of our pre-agreed destiny, reconnecting us to our truth, so whatever happens to us, we would have pre-known. Right down to the different series of events and circumstances that we find ourselves in, allowing us to be more accepting and able to cope, with whatever happens to us. This is the pathway we chose and it's all part of the divine plan, and our continued spiritual growth of our soul.

So what does the future hold for us? The Age of Aquarius is upon us; it demands codes of conduct from us all. With each evolutionary age, come the different trends and cycles. With the Age of Aquarius come a lot of changes, some of which will not be pleasant, but whatever happens we should be prepared for. The Age of Aquarius encourages us to be aware of spirituality, holistic and alternative medicines, the different cultures and your higher consciousness. It's about reinventing and rediscovering your authentic self, to know the truth about the different events that will happen to us, within this lifetime.

The new age of spirituality is about each person empowering him or her, not just to become successful, but to fulfil their deepest dreams and desires. Being able to survive and overcome our difficult times, transforming ourselves and our lives. We can then achieve our full potential in activating our instinctive survival abilities. There are a lot of spiritual traditions and practices readily available, how we choose which path to follow, are up to each individual and to their interests. Spiritual pathways all have one purpose, for they are not just a way of life, they are the different methods of achieving a life, consciously and in doing so, enables us to

144

find our inner-selves through the process of spirituality. We do not find ourselves within the different cultures and techniques, but through them, allowing ourselves the opportunity for spiritual and personal growth.

The twenty-first century has new beginnings for us all; we must find our personal resources to meet the challenges in order to transform ourselves. We must have the courage to set off on the soul's journey, to enable the reconnection with our ultimate power of our truth. The future is about accomplishing our dreams, to be living a life, effortlessly. To be able to achieve our personal inner peace, allowing the vibrations within to radiate outwards into the world, eradicating human suffering and enabling World Peace.

The simple pleasures of life, creates Well Being they also give us quality time with nature, pursuing our interests and talents. When we allow creativity into our daily lives, we are then able to express our truth in all that we say and do. In achieving the reconnection of the higher self and that of our higher consciousness, will allow us to live with balance and harmony, maintaining a healthy mind, body and soul. We can then elevate the stress and tension, granting us with more energy and vitality in pursuing our goals. With determination, strength and the right attitude, we can accomplish anything that we want too. We just need to have faith, belief and trust that the future will hold great things, for us all.

During the Aquarian age we will experience some very hard times, with our lives been thrown into chaos. But the most important fact is about the changes to each individual. We will experience changes to our physical body's energy field, the corresponding effects of the earth's and solar systems energy, all changing due to the magnetic field weakening and reversal of the poles. There are scientists, as well as ancient calendars and tribal prophecies, predicting the end of the world, as we know it. Not necessarily the end of the world full stop, but with catastrophic proportions of our world changing, due to the magnetic field weakening. Within each and every-one of us is a chakra system, meridians lines and acupuncture points. Within the earth's structure is a chakra system, meridian lines and acupuncture points, all of these will dramatically change with the weakening of the magnetic field.

Spirituality is becoming a way of life, to allow us to survive these changes; we must prepare the mind, body and soul. We need to bring our vibrations to a higher level, in order to evolve with these changes and times, allowing ourselves the opportunity of not being left behind. We all need to be able to participate in the spiritual transformation of our world, with us all experiencing great phenomenon as our higher conscious awareness increases, and the opportunities arise to allow us with the clearing of the subconscious or unconscious mind of the repressed and negative emotions. This allows the uplifting of consciousness, with us all becoming a part of the collective consciousness of humankind, once more.

Parallel lives is about bring your consciousness into the future, to project and manifest all that you desire, in doing so, you can improve the outlook not just for yourself, but for others too. We need to actively counterbalance the negativity, help heal human suffering and re-educate ourselves to be less demanding on our resources. We need a collective consciousness to rid our world of the mass negativity. We all have to play our conscious part, firstly achieving it for ourselves, then others. We are re-cycled souls, time travellers, aiming to undo all that we have done or perceived wrongly in the past, which has added to our present climate, with the slow decline of our planet and ourselves. We have brought this on by our constant needs and wants, adding to the demands made upon our natural resources. Maybe our planet is meant to have the natural disasters, to slowly claim back its original origin, an evolutionary cycle. With extinction being a natural part of the earth's journey, to naturally rest, to regenerate and restore balance and harmony, really no difference to that of our soul.

You would think that we would have understood the consequences of our actions by now. But if everything does happen for a reason then maybe the theory is, that with the earth only being a small part of creation, just as we are only a small part of the real us, and with reconnection to the source makes us whole and complete once more, giving us a more collective awareness of what life's all about. With the Age of Aquarius, aids the reconnection of that source and of the higher consciousness, enabling us to achieve our goals and ambitions at a much higher level. When this happens, we accomplish our full potential, becoming a limitless being once more, allowing us to pursue the experiences and adventures of life, to the highest good of all. We must achieve balance within all aspects of our planet and the resources within its structure. Drawing on the Universal energy that sustains all of life and creation, which will serve us all individually and collectively, creating a better future for all.

It was Gods intention that we should live in peace and harmony, but first, we agreed to sort the imbalances out, whether they were personally, to others or to our planet. In achieving our life's purpose, we will accelerate our journey into the twenty-first century, where we can make great changes that will affect the whole of creation. We have no control over the governments and the decisions they make, we can object and express our views, but they will not change anything. The things that we can change, is how we individually perceive the difficult situations and to the way we allow them, to affect us. We do not have to buy into the negativity that comes with the repercussions of their actions. But we can and should address the negativity and to how it affects each individual.

The future holds a lot of uncertainty, but if we allow ourselves the opportunity to reconnect with the truth of the higher consciousness, we would then become much more understanding to what is actually going on. So what is going on? A nation fighting for control, there are no winners, just innocent people losing a fighting battle that they have no control over. All of us becoming the victims to the cause and effect of all actions, but if all of life has a purpose, what is that purpose?

We have experienced many lifetimes fighting for causes that we believed to be right. With the theory that everyone is right in what they do, then no-one is wrong in what they believe or pursue. We all fight for what we believe in, but these beliefs change with every lifetime that we have, in order for us to experience all aspects of life. There are no losers, if we can learn from what life is all about. It's not about fighting political wars, but to conquer the war within, the unrest within our soul. A product of our miss-guided beliefs of fighting for things outside of ourselves that we really do not have any control over. Fighting for a cause where the real truth of what it's all about, is kept from us.

Over the centuries, the unrest of the nation as manifested in world suffering with the veils of deceit keeping us all in the dark. Political battles will always continue because of the controls, our personal battles do not have too. We have freedom; we just did not realise the control that we have over ourselves. To be free, is to give up the things that we have no control over, we are then able to reconnect to the truth that would set us free, from the restraints and restrictions within our life.

The future only holds uncertainty because we have strayed from the source within, to be still and go within, would allow us to become all knowing, with us sensing our truth and purpose in life instinctively. We need to understand that when we have reconnected and become whole once more, we would then become more trusting and accepting of the overall outcome of our planet. Knowing that whatever happens was meant to happen, all being a big part of the divine plan. We must believe that we will become stronger and wiser and that we would be able to cope.

We are living in a dimensional world, there is a lot more going on than we could ever possibly know or even fully understand in a human form. But if the inevitable happened with the destruction of our planet, we must have faith and trust that we would be ensured a place, in the next dimensional realm. To become all knowing, we would have to become all accepting, knowing that everything happens for a reason. We are all required to become our truth, to know the truth about our actions and interactions within every aspect of our lives. We have to believe in ourselves totally, to understand our potential and unique abilities, it's important to have a clear vision of what we want to accomplish and to the reasons why we want to accomplish them.

The future holds great things for us all, but we must first, allow ourselves the opportunity to be open to our life's lessons and to be able to receive the information that's needed in order to learn from them. So let me explain, to know your truth in all situations, allow you to be more accepting of all that happened, good or bad. This allows the positives aspects of those learning's to carry you forwards, through the different challenges that we must experience, as part of our life's path. We must be able to forgive and to surrender all the things that have not been beneficial to our Well Being. Knowing that by becoming an empty vessel allows the universe to give the knowledge and wisdom to you, but more importantly when it is needed.

When we are no longer attached to our thoughts or emotional issues, we will be able to find the solutions to our problems. If you could just image yourself to be empty of any thoughts, beliefs, preconceived ideas, old programming and fears, you would then be in a position, in which to receive the answers to the questions that evades us. When we have achieved a positive mindset, it will allow the mind, body and soul to be influenced by the higher vibration of the higher consciousness, allowing us to be all knowing, naturally.

149

In enlightenment, we would become all forgiving, all accepting, all trusting and to have the faith to know that everyone is living out the different aspects of their own truth. So that we can all overcome the many obstacles within our lives, helping us to achieve Well-being. When we surrender our worries and issues to God, would allow them to be sorted at a higher level of consciousness. Granting us to become free of all restraints, in order to receive all that we need in attaining a healthy life, evolving to a higher vibration where all will be revealed. For future growth, we need to unite with the new vibrations of our planet, a transition from the lower consciousness to the higher consciousness. We could then explore the many pathways of spirituality consciously, transforming our lives allowing us to experience our uniqueness and authentic self. Achieving our dreams, knowing that we are seeking happier times where we can enjoy our accomplishments.

Our future does not have to be all doom and gloom; we can evolve to the higher vibrations so that the negativity does not affect us. In achieving our higher conscious abilities, allows us to walk the earth plane detached from all negative emotions and suffering. This enables our positive nature to counteract some of the negativity, helping others to achieve their goals and ambitions. Actions speak louder than words, positive vibrations influence all those that expose themselves to it, leaving them feeling uplifted and energised. Allowing them to seek what they need successfully and instinctively, in maintaining a state of Well-Being. This then becomes a natural vibration that connects us to the source, of the universe and the power of divinity that sustains all growth.

This is the time of new beginnings for us all, not giving into the uncertainty of what our future holds. To be living in the Now would allow us the opportunity to explore the next evolutionary age with confidence. We will all experience some incredible in-sights into our higher conscious abilities, of the natural gifts of extraordinary phenomenon. With some of us having out of body experiences, astral travel, remote vision, the third eye opening and our altered state of awareness. This allows us to be more accepting of these unique and instinctive gifts of survival, helping us to maintain balance and harmony. There is nothing to fear within these gifts, for they are our natural abilities, the higher vibrations allowing them to become activated so that we can achieve great things naturally. We are pure energy being affected by the changing energy of our planet. We are all participating in the purification and cleansing of our planet, the restoration of balance and harmony.

The year 2012 and the Age of Aquarius was not the end of our world but the beginning, with new skills, talents and abilities, joyfully experiencing our journey of the soul's quest consciously. With this new age we must all rejoice in what we do have within our lives, focusing on our accomplishments and to the people that we hold so dear. So every day in every-way we should be thankful for the pleasures that we all share, reaching out to others. We can offer support and comfort, encouraging then onwards, but also in making sure that we all have everything that we need to maintain health on every level. This will ensure positive growth on our spiritual pathway and for the benefit of future generations to come, where we can all gain the infinite knowledge and wisdom together. I believe that the future is not all doom and gloom; I think we are in for a very exciting and rewarding time, once we overcome the purification and cleansing period. But also to trust that everything within our lives is being overseen by a power, more powerful than anything that we have ever encountered.

The future will allow us the opportunity to gain the greater understanding of our purpose, enabling us to recognise and reach our full potential. We will have died and be reborn again, maybe many times before our planet earns it's rest, the distinction of life as we know it. But more importantly, we have all got time to make a difference to the souls continued journey of the completion and the reconnection of the higher self and consciousness. We could live on this planet with very little resources, as long as we were no longer depending on the things outside of ourselves, for survival.

Our inner resources can sustain a healthy, happy and contented life, once we had reconnected to them. Not just achieving great wealth but abundance within and throughout our lifetime. This will allow us to use the infinite power of our achievements in other future incarnate forms.

The overall journey in the completion of the soul enables us to become All Knowing that the collective consciousness would become All Encompassing everything and everyone eventually returning to the source of Divinity. This allows us to become whole and complete once more, having completed yet another cycle, and then waiting for the cycle of evolution to start all over again.

CONCLUSION

Parallel lives connect us to our own infinite vibration, of which we've always been. Travelling through each incarnated existence, the Souls quest of continuance is to reconnect with the ultimate power of the whole of creation. Life is about our vibrational source, attracting all that we need, whether its people, situations, or the different circumstances of our life's lessons, our pre-destined agreed learning's.

We are a vibration, the level of which was set at birth, the agreed conscious level of our abilities that will naturally attract all that we need within our lives, helping us to understand the lessons that we have agreed too. The understandings of which will allow our vibrations to expand and evolve, granting us the ultimate Knowledge and Wisdom that will sustain our future growth. We all aspire to the vibration of the higher consciousness, expanding the mind's energy to enable the comprehension of the possibilities that we open ourselves up too. This allows the higher self to excel in every area of our lives, to become a vibrational force that only attracts the positive aspects in all that we do. Bring the positive skills, gifts, talents and abilities from all lifetimes, into this one. This helps us to achieve all that we desire, and our dreams and ambitions being manifested to the highest good of all.

Do not deny ourselves the opportunity in claiming back our true power, giving us the chance to really know, who we truly are, and we are unique in every possible way, but more importantly, we're the power of our thoughts, deeds and actions, a part of our true essence, and the vibration of our soul, that holds a true record of who we really are, and too whom we have ever been, but more importantly, the person that we have now become.

If you would like to get in touch with me, to express your views or experiences I would love to hear from you. I hope you have enjoyed my latest book and it has left you wanting to know more. I look forward to hearing from you, good luck and every success in the future.

Website:

www.veronicalavendersholisticevents.co.uk

www.veronicalavender.com

Email: veronicalavender@btinternet.com

70900409R00093

Made in the USA
Columbia, SC
20 May 2017